Bill Hoatson Presents
" Professor Johnson's"

Life Lessons

Bill Hoatson Presents
" Professor Johnson's"

Life Lessons

Bill Hoatson

ARPress
ILLUMINATING IDEAS
EMPOWERING VOICES

ARPress
45 Dan Road Suite 5
Canton MA 02021

Hotline:1(888) 821-0229
Fax:1(508) 545-7580

Ordering Information:
Quantity sales. Special discounts are available on quantity purchases by corporations, associations, and others. For details, contact the publisher at the address above.

Printed in the United States of America.

ISBN-13:   Paperback   979-8-89356-044-2
              eBook   979-8-89356-045-9

Library of Congress Control Number: 2024903342

TABLE OF CONTENTS

FOREWORD

Bill Hoatson has been an educator for 40 years in economically depressed areas of North Florida and Southern Georgia. He has taught and enriched the lives of thousands of white, black and Hispanic students at every grade level. He has taught in pre-k, elementary school, middle school, high school and vocational school, both regular and exceptional education. His vast experience has given him deep insights into getting the best out of each and every child. This is important for all children, but especially valuable for those who come from disadvantaged or stressed backgrounds or those with learning disabilities. His books and lectures are both penetrating and entertaining. He should be read by anybody interested in the emotional and academic success of children.

"Life Lessons" is about parenting. Over the decades the author has seen firsthand not only the profound importance of the role of parents in child development but how early childhood experiences from birth to four will impact a child for the rest of his or her life. Though society often looks to the classroom as if it were the first training-place of little minds and characters, we know that what happens to a child before the school years directly affects how that child will do in school, shaping for better or worse what their adult lives will be like. And he realized with increasing dismay that most people don't begin to understand how critically important the years from birth to four are for everything that will happen in a child's life.

Bill Hoatson has taught generations of students in the same families—the children of the children of the children—as each has grown into adulthood. So when he is teaching his concern is not just for the child in front of him, but for that child's future children as well. He knows that how well he does for this child will be passed down as he or she parents his or her own children.

But what happens when parents aren't very good at parenting? That is the question that keeps Bill up at night. That is the reason for this book.

Bill believes that no matter how badly they may handle the job, nobody actually wants to be a bad parent. His philosophy of "judge not that you be not judged" supports a steady flow of positive communication between him and parents, communication that can be very helpful to children. He also understands compassionately the pressures that can weigh on parents, and there is a long list of them—households mired in poverty or joblessness, families headed by one parent struggling alone, the unpreparedness of very young parents barely out of childhood themselves, households steeped in anger or hopelessness, emotionally damaged individuals who are coping with life the best they can. Indeed, wherever he sees parents who fall short, he sees people "coping with life the best they can."

So Bill's first purpose in this book is to help parents cope better, to give them the skills to be good parents, no matter what their background and life experience. His message is that anybody can do it. Anybody can build a confident, intelligent, academically capable child, including those children with learning or physical challenges. Anybody.

But his deeper purpose is to break the generational cycle in households that aren't doing so well. How in the world, he asks, can a child raised in a dysfunctional home be expected to know how to be a good parent to his or her own children? He has seen families where academic failure, emotional instability, or even incarceration seem to be generational, handed down like a bad habit. But he also knows that these families aren't saddled with a "failure gene" or "crime gene." What they need is a map of a path out of the woods.

It is his belief that ultimately the best remedy for parenting mistakes is to give this parenting course to every single tenth grader in America—before they have children—to break the cycle. But parenting is inherently difficult even if you were well parented or are parenting your sixth child, because each child is a new experience and a new challenge. This book will instill the confidence in any would-be parent that they can actually do this right.

The beauty of the book is that it will be readily absorbed and retained, especially by young readers, because it is entertaining and funny. One of his students in an admiring letter said 'Mr. Hoatson is uplifting, funny and likes joking around. He takes our problems to heart, and is there to help in any way he can with our work, etc. He makes us laugh and learning is fun." I believe that perfectly sums up both Bill and his book.

Emanuel Shargel
Professor Emeritus
College of Education, Florida State University

ADDRESSING STUDENTS

School systems would occasionally call Professor Johnson to come speak to troubled students. He would never turn them down, insisting to his college professor colleagues that it was "real teaching," unlike what transpired on campus. He would chide them that it was infinitely easier to teach kids who had actually paid money for it than those with one foot in the failure bucket.

Professor Johnson once explained that to change a kid's behavior you don't tiptoe around issues in which they are already engaged. If they are going to act grown, then talk to them like they're grown. In order for them to actually listen to you they need to trust three things: your motivation for speaking, your knowledge of what you are talking about, and the honesty with which it is delivered. And it better be funny.

Once Professor Johnson was asked if he was ever disappointed at the amount of students who didn't seem to take his lectures to heart. He responded that he was always pleased and amazed at how many that actually did. On the following pages he takes head-on issues that greatly impact society: violence, teen pregnancy, and successful parenting skills. In the words of one of his ex-students, "Professor Johnson delivers." We can't print what he really said, but it was complimentary.

Introduction To Professor Johnson's Infamous Lecture On Parenting

It has been my pleasure to have been a teacher in various capacities for what seems like the last eighty years. I have taught elementary school for five years, exceptional education with teenagers for sixteen years. I have been a behavioral specialist and had a hand in developing an academy for a school district, where we accept children that are expelled from the school system and try to turn their lives around. I have been the acting discipline coordinator for the same school system. In that capacity I would find myself sitting in a juvenile courtroom every Thursday, student records in my lap, watching my children go to jail. They were all good kids, but they all had done really bad things. And most of them came from families so dysfunctional that they didn't stand a chance at home, in school, in the courtroom, or in society. They were not bad families. These were not evil people; they just didn't possess one shred of any kind of proper parenting tools. When mom shows up in court with her bedroom slippers on, curlers in her hair, standing next to her son whose underwear is showing from underneath his "Cocaine is the breakfast of champions" T-shirt, this is not a good sign. They need help. Their children need help. Locking a child in a cage is not help. It may be necessary for society, but it does not go under the heading of helpful services. It is my hope that this lecture, as lightweight as it is, will be of service to somebody, somewhere. The question is, how do you create children that can succeed in school and in life?

While most schools are wonderful places for children to be, staffed by true heroes in our society, I realize full well that a lot of schoolwork is dull; some teachers couldn't teach their way out of a paper bag and some administrators shouldn't be in charge of a pet, much less a student. This being said, I have also found that if a child is seriously struggling in school and exhibiting behavioral problems, which often go hand in hand, that there is often a child rearing struggle in the background that greatly magnifies whatever shortcomings that could be found in the school. The good news is that you can prepare your child for a successful life, NO MATTER WHAT KIND OF SCHOOL HE ATTENDS.

The secret of a child's success in school is what happens to them from conception to five years old. I do not like to use terms like "properly" when talking about child rearing, because they carry the baggage of moral judgment. Lord only knows there is enough judgment of child rearing practices, or lack there-of, to go around. And around again. I will say that a five year old raised effectively is light years ahead of one raised ineffectively and is already miles down the road to success where the other child is still trying to find his driveway. The main thrust of this lecture is that no matter what the child's background, race, creed, color, religious affiliation, political party, gender, hairstyle or solar system they come from they can ALL succeed in school and in life if they are groomed for success. This is a child success grooming talk. Regardless of what kind of school your child goes to, YOU hold the keys to their success. Think about that for a while before you jump for joy.

Being the key holder is liberating and scary at the same time. Professor Johnson is here to help with the liberating part and evaporate the scary part. Child rearing has been going on for thousands of years. It is not rocket science. What makes child rearing scary these days is not the child or the rearing. It's the "these days" that we're all having a problem with, parents and teachers alike. Welcome to the brave new world of raising successful children. This lecture serves as a roadmap. At least my publisher hopes so. She's counting on it, even as she eyes me warily.

Bill Hoatson

Professor Johnson's Infamous Lecture On Parenting: How To Create The Successful Child

PREFACE

Professor Johnson's lecture on parenting-for-success was given at an In-House Suspension Room at Barkley High School in the spring of 2004. All of the students in attendance were there as part of their rehabilitation program for sexually active, underage teenagers.

It is a pleasure to be here at Barkley High on a Saturday morning, even if this is the indoor suspension room. Some of my best lectures have been in ISS rooms. There's nothing like a captive audience. Now, if I look at my note card correctly, I see that we are here to talk about sex today. What a great way to start out a Saturday!

Usually, my talks are given to groups of students who deal with their problems by beating people up. The only time sex comes into the discussion is when we get to the part about life in prison. That is, if you call dead silence a discussion. So it's great to be amongst a bunch of young people who don't want to hurt anybody, they just want to get their groove on. Young lady, how old are you? . . . 16? . . . Young lady, how old are you? . . . 14? . . . Young man? . . . 15? Young man? . . . . 15? Let me ask you something. Do you think sex is natural or unnatural? . . . . How about you? . . . Young lady, would you characterize sex as fun or not fun? . . . How about you? . . . . Did you realize there was a study done that shows how often your average human being has some kind of a sexual thought? For males its like once every thirty seconds, or some such crazy number. To sum up, sex is natural, it's fun as all get out, and everybody thinks about it all the time. On top of this, we live in a society where, I don't care what you're selling, there's an underclothed woman somewhere nearby. So, you are locked up on this beautiful Saturday morning for what? For being human? I say this is an outrage! This is an injustice. What were they thinking about? I shall call the principal first thing Monday morning and give him a piece of my mind. Class dismissed. Let's go home.

Wait. Wait a minute. Please return to your seats. I almost forgot something. Thank you. I forgot to introduce a couple of very important visitors. Mrs. Wilson, could you please send your daughter up here, while I sit for a second? . . . What's your name sweetheart? . . . . Shonterica? That's a beautiful name. Your parents have imagination. My name is Bill. How old are you? . . . 4? What's your favorite food? . . . Chicken? Mine, too. What time is dinner? . . . What do you mean you don't know? It's when I get there is when. Why don't you sit in my lap for a second? Now, Mrs. Woodbury, would you escort your reluctant son up here please? Hi, there young man. What's your name? . . . I can't hear you while your face is in your mother's dress . . . .

Robert? A very manly name. How old are you, Robert? Hold them up high and let me count. One, two, three. Three years old and no gray hair yet. How do you do it? And what is your favorite food? . . . . What's that? I can't quite make it out, but I think he said get me away from this crazy man before I cry. I want to thank you, Shonterica and Robert, for visiting me for a minute. It was a joy. Let's give them a round of applause, please. Thank you, Mrs. Williams, Mrs. Woodbury, for coming this morning. Bye.

You know, it dawned upon me that you're not in this room, on a Saturday, because of your interest in sex. You are here because of Shonterica and Robert . . . Of course having two little children here was a set up. Let's call it a visual aid. Weren't they cool? Nothing cuter than a little child, if only they'd stay that way. You are here because of a large societal fear that if you have a Shonterica or a Robert, and are too immature to raise them properly, terrible things can happen to them. Did you see little Robert there, clinging to his mother? That child is totally dependent on her. The power that mother has over her child is terrifying. She can do anything to that child that she wants. She could beat him, starve him, abuse him, yell at him, lock him in a closet, torture him, neglect him, kill him. It's easy. There is not one single thing that child could do about it. As a parent, you have total power over another human being.

I remember being married—way too young, by the way—living in a crowded trailer park, which is what happens when you get married way too young, because you don't have any money. I was surrounded by young couples in the same circumstances, except some had babies. I remember this young man shrieking at his baby each night, cursing at it, trying desperately to make it stop crying. Then there were the sounds of him beating the baby. I cried myself to sleep for two nights before I got up the courage to call the police.

I don't know if the young man was evil or mentally ill. I have the horrible feeling that he was normal, except crushed by the weight of the awesome responsibility of caring for a human being, for which he was totally unprepared. Years later I do remember seeing my own infant son laying propped up on some pillows and almost fainting from the sheer magnitude of the responsibility and the overwhelming feeling of helplessness, both his and mine.

So, in the end, it is society's knowledge and fear of bad parenting that drives many of the sex laws between consenting, but also UNDERAGE people, meaning in your case, children. Now, I understand full well that many of you will have sex, no matter what I say. I could easily spend an hour on the hundred and one ways to PREVENT pregnancy. The fact is, you DO need to listen to that lecture, and listen carefully. I have found, however, that the best way to prevent pregnancy is to understand the enormity of the job of parenting. THAT understanding will not only drive you to go to a lecture on pregnancy prevention, but sit bolt-upright through it, because you are actually paying close attention. So I am going to conduct a class on parenting today. You're stuck with me for two hours, so you might as well get something out of it.

I have four goals in mind. One, is to instill in you the seriousness of child rearing so that it might change your reckless sexual behavior. Two, is to create a conceptual framework to work from so that you are not driven by fear or ignorance to do crazy things to your own child. Three, is to give you the tools to help create a glorious adulthood for your child. If done right, you can give your child a large head start on being a success in life. It is my firm belief that all children have great destinies. It is your job as parent to set the stage for their greatness. And, four, is to have a little fun. I don't see this as a wasted Saturday. This could be the best Saturday of your life . . . . What are you moaning about? By your behavior you were begging for a parenting class. Well, ask and ye shall receive. What a miraculous world we live in! You can just be thankful that this isn't a Lamaze class.

Now, to begin. I brought several charts with me today. The first over here is the title of my lecture: "How to Raise Your Child to be a Success in Life Instead of Being Headed for Jail or a Violent, Possibly Drug-Addled, Death." Catchy, huh? Next is a list of the fifteen topics we'll cover.

Since sex is where it all begins, that's where we'll start. Rule number one is, parenting is for responsible adults only. A child cannot raise a child properly. Half of the adults out there can't either. It is the single hardest thing you'll ever do in your life. If you asked the man who conquered Mount Everest what his greatest feat was, he would not even mention anything that had to do with mountains, unless it was the mountain of debt had accumulated for the college fund. Child rearing is deeply rewarding at times, but if anybody ever describes child rearing as fun, head for the exit, because the person is deeply disturbed, and possibly dangerous.

Now, I know you think you're grown. It is not your body that society is worried about, however. It's your brain. Are you capable of making adult choices? The short answer is ARE YOU KIDDING ME? Every brain has a corpus callosum. When it connects both sides of the brain it creates an organ capable of higher order, or adult thinking. The problem is, this doesn't happen until between 17 and 22 years old. Ever see one of your bright, intelligent friends do something really stupid? And you're going, "What was he thinking about?" Who knows? To the immature brain it seemed like a really cool idea at the time. Looking back at their own childhood, most adults are just happy to be alive, much less be a success. So society has passed laws that may punish you for having sex under18, because they KNOW you are not ready for parenthood. It's like giving a driver's license to a ten year old. The fact that he's big for his age and his foot reaches the peddle is besides the point.

Now, my own personal opinion is, if you're not ready to raise a child properly, you are not ready for sex. I don't care what age you are. A clue is if you engage in child thinking vs. adult thinking. The number one indicator is how self-centered you are. An infant is completely and totally self-centered. I'm hungry, I'm tired, I want, I, I, I. An adult factors in others and asks different questions, such as: Are you hungry? Are you tired? What can I do for you? Don't ever have a birthday party catered by two year olds. You will go home not having had any fun and hungry, because they will share NOTHING with the guests. You should check your own self-centered meter. I had a pregnant student who had her meter stuck way over on "I." She was telling her girlfriends that her grandmother was going to raise her child for her so that she could achieve her life's goal: to go to the club and party a lot. I also give a separate lecture on what to do when grandma goes off the deep end and agrees, but that's for another time.

More subtly, I had a long, rather enlightening conversation with a young man, who was soon to be a dad. He talked about getting his child the finest things in life. He told me that if his boy wanted a $200 pair of shoes he would steal them for him if he had to. I asked him why, and he told me that his kid deserved as much as any rich kid. I admired that attitude, but asked him, what if you went to jail in the process? He said that he didn't care if he went to jail for ten years, his child was going to have the best. I let that sit for a moment and then I asked him if he really thought that his child would rather have a pair of shoes, or even gold or diamonds, than his own father? Sadly, his idea of fatherhood remained with giving things. The truth is, what a child wants and needs is you. Your love, your TIME. And lots of it. That's why it's so hard for a lot of people to be good parents. You can't just give your way to good parenthood. The question becomes, are you and your partner willing to be on duty, 24/7, for the next 18 years of your life, not that you even really know what happens in 18 years of life. And in that 24/7 duty time, willing to devote large chunks of it to actually being with your child.

You noticed that I mentioned the word partner? Don't think for 30 seconds that you don't need one. Let's take a look at the next chart, which is the sex and money chart. Doesn't get much better than this in America, does it? Sex and money. I want you to take special note of this line here, which is taking a 75 degree nose dive into the ground. That's the single parent poverty death spiral. This 90 degree plunging line over here is the single parent with no diploma suicide drop. And this next chart, here, shows the number of young men under 20 who are willing to get married and stick with their sex partner once she becomes pregnant . . . . What's that? . . . Yes, I know that it's blank. Young men, I want you to look around the room and notice that you are the only ones laughing. Ladies, you know that frosty look you just gave Mr. Happy sitting next to you? You might want to use that a little more when they're throwing whatever passes for charm these days your way. Eighty-five percent of all households in poverty are headed by single parent women. This partner thing is huge and impacts the children in hundreds of different ways.

What happens when there is a pregnancy? You have three options. You and your partner can do what-ever it takes to flip your self-centered needle way over to the adult side, act as a team, and set about the business of successful child rearing. This leads directly to our next topic, which is prenatal care.

Or, men, you can run and pretend you don't have a child. You can pretend like you don't even know the mother, couldn't pick her out of a police lineup. But in reality that pretend family of yours is going to go into the tank, and it's all your fault, and you know it.

What separates the men from the boys and the women from the girls is not the sex act. Any fool, if lucky enough, can do that. It's how you react to the word pregnant. Wishful thinking, pretending and running away are all highly valued tools that a child uses to deal with reality, but are the kiss of death to an adult. Which side do you fall on? If you fall on the adult side, let's start looking at the concrete steps for creating a successful child, from the day after, "Honey, I'm pregnant!" If you fall on the child side and feel completely overwhelmed, and unequipped to deal with having a child, there are lots of agencies set up to help. Go to them. That's what they are there for. That is option three.

The building of a successful child starts from day one of the pregnancy. And the strength of the team will be tested one minute after that. That's right guys, you don't have 9 months to sit around and decide if you're joining the team or not. The team is hitting the field NOW. Job one for each team member is to answer the question, "Do I want this child?" This step is crucial, because the phrase, "Honey, I'm pregnant," does not always result in squeals of delight. This and the bankruptcy thing are the two real team killers. If you don't know the answer, go join Superman in his fortress of solitude, and don't come out until you do. Do whatever mental gymnastics it takes, because if the child is not wanted then you are not going to be willing to make the sacrifices necessary to raise a child properly. The baby does not care in the least if it is planned. It has a huge interest in being loved and wanted, however. If you can get to where you can say, "I want the baby" in the mirror and keep a straight face without the support of a Jack Daniels bottle, then you are halfway home to being a good parent. The rest of this will be as easy as drinking water.

Now begins the prenatal care phase: raising a child for success inside the mother's body. First, let's look at the next chart. This is fascinating. It shows the different stages of fetal development in the womb, every six weeks. You can see the skeletal development, lung development. Over here is enormous brain development.

A couple rules of thumb: The fetus is part of mom, directly attached to mom through the umbilical cord. Whatever mom eats, fetus eats. Mom drinks, fetus drinks. Mom breathes, fetus breathes. See your doctor about what is best to eat, drink and breathe. The proper diet during the proper six weeks time frame will go a long way to having a child with a properly developed brain that will function efficiently at school. You are now building a college graduate.

I used the word sacrifice a little while ago and saw some of you squirm in your seats. If you think sacrifice is a curse word then that should tell you something about yourself. It means the needle on your self-centered meter is way over to the left, stuck in child mode. There is nothing wrong with that, per se, just don't risk having children by having sex.

So here come the sacrifices. Ladies, no alcohol, cigarettes, drugs, junk food, violence or anger during pregnancy. Eat properly, take your vitamins, see your doctor, and get plenty of sleep. You with me on this? Sometimes it helps to actually hang this chart on a wall somewhere in your house so that you can visually see why you're doing without all this stuff that you should be doing without anyway. It helps your determination. Men, you can help your partner greatly with this by following the same rules. What do you mean WHAT? You think it helps your team mate, who is chewing on the furniture to alleviate her tobacco cravings, to look outside and see you blowing smoke rings out in the front yard. "Hey baby, you want a cold one?" and you throw her a pineapple juice while you pull the tab on a tall Budweiser. No, Buddy-Ro, that's not going to fly. Young lady, pass this bag back to the father-to-be in purple. It looks like he's going to be sick. What's that? . . . I hear you. I don't blame you. Yes, sir? . . . While the abortion option is there, my only reaction to that is that's easy for a man to say. Plus, we're talking about successful child rearing practices today, so we're assuming that there actually is a child to practice on. Whew, sex is serious business. We might as well stay serious for a couple of more minutes. Back to the chart: young lady, let's say you are a heroin addict and have got to shoot up. GOT to. Which six weeks period would you pick to do the least harm? . . . What do you mean it's a lousy choice? Of course it's a lousy choice. I had a girl one time say in the first six weeks, because there was less to mess up. As you correctly deduced by looking at the chart, there is no optimum time for destroying your child.

I have taught for almost 30 years, many of which were spent with children with learning or behavioral disabilities. Do not set your child up for a lifetime of being in the principal's office explaining why he was terrorizing the classroom when, in fact, he couldn't sit still if he wanted to because his entire central nervous system was rewired due to massive amounts of drugs or alcohol. Set your child up for success instead, with good prenatal care. Once the child is born, he's now got a great foundation to grow from: he's loved, and he's healthy, and he's born into a focused, functioning, FAMILY UNIT for support.

Now that you actually have a child, the next step is nutrition. Again . . . Yes, ma'am, what's that? . . . What are we doing? This is a new concept. It is called planning for the future. Even better, proactively shaping the future. It's the vision thing, which, if I'm not mistaken, is number two on the list separating adult thinking from child thinking . . . . This makes your head hurt? Well, the learning process is prone to doing that every once in a while. Just watch. You'll love this. I'll show you how to raise a genius just by shopping. Well, don't get too excited. I'm talking about grocery shopping.

In order for a body and a brain to function properly it must get the right nutrients. Sounds simple enough. A person needs to be fed. The problem is, half of the food in the grocery store is not food, in any real sense of the word. I have never seen a country with so much wealth where people don't eat for survival, but for entertainment. I can see a guy from Bangladesh talking to a U.S. citizen: "What are you eating?" "Just junk. They call it junk food." "Oh, I'm so sorry. I didn't realize it was so bad over here." "No, that's OK. I eat this on purpose." "Oh, do you now?" he says as he slowly backs away from the deranged American. Let's put this into an equation. Junk food equals junk brain, and junk body, which equals fat, bloated, idiot death. The real axis of evil is sugar, grease and salt. Some genius figured out how to take the cheapest commodities on the planet and turn them into gold. You cannot grow one single brain cell with sugar, grease, or salt. Earth to mom and dad. You are not feeding your child for amusement sake only. Building a good brain and body better factor in there somewhere. If you start early, it's easy. My daughter avoids sugar laden cereal because, starting around two years old, I would walk her up and down the cereal aisle and tell the story of the soulless corporate billionaire. This man's sole purpose in life was to make lots of money. He didn't have the spine to be a crack dealer nor the stomach to be a hit man, so he settled on selling chocolate donut cereal to helpless children instead. If they would sell sugar and fat laden products to children to bilk their parents out of their money before their child dies, what else are they capable of doing? Are there no limits to their depravity and greed? Variations of this little fable also works wonders in the snack food aisle or your local "music" store.

Your average child, after getting this over the top response from parent EVERY TIME they ask for something harmful, will not ask anymore. "Put that garbage back on the shelf quick, before dad sees you. Don't get him started!" After awhile, they won't even think about asking, which is exactly what you want. Get the stuff off their radar screen.

It "tastes good" or its "nasty" has a lot more to do with what a child is used to than how food actually tastes. I have seen children dump trays full of good meals, calling it "nasty" and then eating chips or candy bars the rest of the day. Your first line of defense is your home. The first few years of life give you a chance to set up habits that will last your child a lifetime. This difference between "nasty" or "good" is simply what a child has experienced.

A good place to start is NEVER use sugar or candy as a reward for ANYTHING. Don't have any junk food inside your house. When the child opens the refrigerator she sees applesauce, fruits, carrot sticks, yogurt, whole grain breads and peanut butter. Whatever. These are the treats they run for, because that's all there is. And if you treat them like treats they become treats, especially if you actually use the word "treat" when handing it to them. Once you form a habit of eating right, it will stick, or at least be there to fall back on later in life. I know this is sacrilege, but sodas, candy and chips are not food. If you were left on an island with only sodas, candy and chips the rescue team three years later would find a 300 pound dead person with a misspelled plea for help next to him. And I'm willing to bet that he was hyperactive right up to the bitter end. I am not going to beat this nutrition thing to death, but it is crucial when you are building a child for success that you use the right materials. And food is one of the few things that you can actually control, at least at home. You can build a car using plastic and cardboard, I suppose, just don't expect it to run efficiently or last very long. Here's a little ditty you can remember for vegetables: something orange, something green, your brain percolates like a well oiled computing machine; only sugar, only something sweet, that shrunk up little brain will have to take a back seat, it can't compete, it can't perform an intelligent feat . . . Thank you for the applause, but why don't we save it for the dirty jokes at the end.

OK. We've now got a real, live child who is loved and healthy. We are going to get very specific on what a parent can do to facilitate the big three: language, reading and math. We'll take language first. Language rule one: the more quantity of words that a child hears from birth to four, the more you are building a child's brain for language and reading ability. You have permission to drink lots of coffee and chatter away like a magpie in an amphetamine lab. Talk to and around your child a lot, from day one. It doesn't matter in the least that your child doesn't respond and you feel like a fool. The more the better. If you are a frustrated actor, writer, or stand-up comic, let it out. Stand at the crib and do Shakespeare. Try out your rotten comedy routines as you change out a diaper. The worst you'll get are smiles and goo-goos, which is a heck of a lot better than the usual reaction you'll get from drunken adults at nightclubs.

Shut up is not a conversation. If you are unloved, overworked, underpaid, undervalued, unhealthy, trapped in a lousy relationship, or just plain mean: in other words, if your life is so stressed that the least little thing sets you off, get a pet instead of a child. And don't go for the dog, because they require way too much work. Start with a goldfish.

Shut up! Be quiet! I don't want to hear a sound! Well, Mr. I wish my child was a rock instead of a human being, you should have thought of that before you decided to get your freak on. Lots of language, in a normal tone of voice is important for the brain. Yelling and screaming don't count.

Besides quantity, variety is important. The more different words that a child hears from birth, the more complex brain development you will get. If I were to take the top off of an adult's head and took the brain out, what would it look like? . . . A squiggly mess? That's exactly correct. And the more squiggles the better because they are learning and retrieving informational paths. A newborn's brain is fairly smooth. What you don't want is a 16 year old to have the brain wrinkles of a billiard ball. So build vocabulary. Take the stroller up to a flower and start naming the parts. Ignore the fact that all your child really can do is drool well. Go for it. If you don't know anything your own self, drag a dictionary around with you. That's what I do. When you see somebody coming, bend over and say, "I am going to circumvent the corrosive effects of profane language upon your intellect by heaping voluminous amounts of positive adjectives on your little brilliant head." Which will elicit the usual "What?" from your limited vocabulary friends. Occasionally, you will have a friend whose vocabulary is not so limited, who will answer, "What the bleep?!" instead. Let's talk profanity for a minute. This language acquisition thing is great, but there are certain words that you don't want your child to acquire. These, unfortunately, are the ones that are picked up in a millisecond. You can work on the word symphony all you want, but if the child hears the word "bleep," that's all you're going to get. If you're lucky you might get, "Boy, that was a great bleeping symphony." Nowadays, however, it's not just your mouth or your friend's mouth that you have to watch out for. There is an entire industry making millions off of turning your child into a disrespectful, criminal, moron. Don't play this "musical entertainment" around them. A hint is if the title has the word "nasty" in it, like "You're Momma's Got a Nasty New Boyfriend," or "Big Nasty Booty." These are not children's songs on the par of "It's a Small World After All". Now, before you get on your high horse, I'm not telling you what to do. I'm telling you what to do around your child. Big and important difference. Your days of thinking about just number one are just about over. If you look closely, the number one is now on a T-shirt being worn by your child, number two is on your spouse's shirt, numbers three through eight are on other family members and nine through fifteen belong to colleagues at work. Welcome to the adult world. You're lucky if your shirt has a number in double digits.

If you have given your child the proper foundation for language skills: quantity, quality, and variety, the foundation is also laid for reading, WHICH IS THE SINGLE MOST IMPORTANT SKILL THAT A CHILD CAN HAVE. It is also relatively easy to impart, as are most skills if you have the one, single attribute besides love that separates all good parents and teachers from the mediocre: that is patience. If you don't have any, go to the store and buy some, because you're going to need it. Buy it in the giant, economy sized pack.

How fascinating is it, exactly, to sound out d . . . . o . . . . g . . . . dog, for the 48th time? To write the letter "o" over and over again, until done properly? Your child needs you to have the capacity to be bored out of your mind and not show it. You can't fidget, look exasperated, or get angry, because the little brain that is apparently processing information slower than the garden slug that it was inspecting earlier, is going as fast as it can. If you add fear or hostility into the mix, it will not only slow down, but stop. If you think you were frustrated at slow, you'll go ballistic at dead stop. Don't think of a child as a little human being, but as a little mule. What you don't want is for the mule to plant itself, braying for all the world to hear, and refuse to move. This is what you will get if you don't exhibit PATIENCE while a child is learning. There is a little town in Georgia that celebrates Mule Day every year. Well, it will be mule day around your house every day if you don't let learning happen at its natural pace, following its natural course.

What is the natural course? For reading, you simply place the child on your lap, starting with the ride home from the hospital, and read a book. Every night. THAT'S ALL. It does not take a rocket scientist to teach reading. It takes time and patience. The child's brain is naturally going to absorb the process. It will figure out that in America, we read from left to right and top to bottom. That we turn pages. That letters make sounds. That a period is a stop sign. That reading is enjoyable. As the baby gets a little older, you start pointing out what sounds each letter makes, or each blend. You point to key words like "cat" or "jump," and have the child read the whole word. After a few years—the patience thing—the child is reading to YOU. And this is all before a child enters school. They will not only be school ready, but set up to excel in it.

DO NOT EXPECT THE SCHOOL TO TEACH YOUR CHILD TO READ. If you wait until school age to introduce your child to reading, your child is already five years behind everybody else when he enters school and will struggle his whole life to catch up. I cannot stress this enough. A teacher with a one-to-twenty ratio, at best, is not able to do what a parent, who is one-on-one, can do with a child. Not even close. And it's not their job to fill a five year void, because while they're doing that, the child is missing what he currently should be getting.

You, as parent, can ensure your child's success. That is the good news. When they are very young get the baby cloth books, which are made for chewing on. Then let them chew it and enjoy the book. Help them make their own books as they get older. They love this. They get to use paper, staplers, glue, crayons, rulers, pencils, pens, markers, computers, whatever. They also get to do the artwork and book format. Being an author of a book, even one that only has three words on each page, is an empowering thing for a child. It is the joy of reading times two, because it adds the element of performance to it, with adult approval as a reward, which is a giant incentive. Let them read their books to you, their grandmother, the traveling salesperson that you are trying to get rid of. It doesn't matter. The adult approval that they will receive for their intellectual abilities is worth its weight in gold. The child feels that his power base is centered in his brain. This is exactly where you want your child to feel powerful, because there are a lot of negative power sources, which we'll discuss later. I once ran a behavioral class for violent 4th and 5th graders. Most were reading on a kindergarten or first grade level. We would make our own books and learn to read them. If they behaved themselves that day their reward was to walk down to the office and read out loud to the principal, secretary, janitor or any willing adult that they could rustle up. It was like magic. These children would do ANYTHING to stay out of trouble so that they could go show off their reading. It was the highlight of their day. It was definitely the highlight of the adult's day to watch these children beaming with pride at their intellectual accomplishments. This was the raw power of positive attention at its best. I have found that if children get enough positive attention then they won't spend their energy doing outrageous things to get your attention in a negative way. The bottom line is, they are going to get attention one way or the other. Which do you prefer? The beauty of giving and getting positive attention for reading is that after a while it becomes a self-generating positive energy machine, because the act of reading itself is so rewarding on its own. It is also the one intellectual gift, if you had only one to give, that will help your child succeed in life above all others. So give it. It is yours to give. Just make sure that the child is having fun with words. And that you and other adults are part of that fun.

Give books as gifts and make a big deal out of getting one. Give reading in the disguise of games, like crossword puzzles and spelling dice. When they get older, have a family reading time of at least one half hour, where they read for pleasure every day. Read books yourself and let junior see you do it. This is critical and, judging by the moaning and groaning, means another radical lifestyle change for some of you. I'm going to give you an insight into parenting that will last you a lifetime. The secret is that no child wants to be a child. They all want to be grown. The only people who actually want to be children are adults. They have seen both sides of the equation and have figured that children, by far, have the better deal. Children have not seen both sides of the equation yet, so they spend all their efforts towards what they see as the better deal: being a grown-up.

There is one powerful phrase that a parent needs to keep in the fore part of their mind. It is also my entire drug lecture, which I'll give right now: MONKEY SEE, MONKEY DO. That explains everything. That's it. If you want your child to read, you read. If you want her to be a profanity spewing, ax wielding alcoholic, then that is what you model. A family reunion would be a perfect time for this. Children spend their whole life aspiring to be you, to be an adult.

The power of the parent to shape a child, for good or bad, is awesome, even to an adult in their forties. It is overwhelming for one who is too young, particularly because parenting has a lot to do with YOU and how YOU conduct yourself. If you are not willing to make personal changes for the betterment of another human being, then don't put yourself in the position of being a parent. In case any of this sounds familiar, you may consider it a THEME, which may come in handy if you have to write a paper on this for school. You've prepared your child for language use and reading. Now it's math time. A lot of math tasks stimulate a different part of the brain than reading tasks, so we need to do different preps than the reading and language preps. One thing as a parent is real easy. Get your child a bunch of blocks and let them play. Building things with their hands develops a certain spatial sense, which is half of what higher math is anyway.

Small children need a sense of one-to-one correspondence. Ask your child how many chairs are in the room, and have them touch the chair as they are counting. Kids love this. Children learn through touching. Their need to touch is somewhat akin to that of Uncle Fred's tobacco need when he is out of cigarettes. It is an absolute necessity. Don't have the mentality of the owner of an expensive antique store in your house. On this note, you do realize that you are going to have to child-proof your entire house, which means barring the doors to everything dangerous and placing everything else at least ten feet off the ground. Once the child learns to crawl, it's fifteen feet.

Play spatial games, such as dot-to-dot, checkers, or chess. Have them do puzzles. Play dice games. Play anything that has numbers in it. Dust off the old roulette wheel and see how he does. This could be useful later in case the college thing doesn't go so well. There are a ton of ways a simple BINGO set up can be used.

Give a small earned allowance to instill knowledge of money. As the child gets older, realistic money based problems are a motivator for learning proper math skills, like "I don't have any idea where you are going to get fifty bucks, but your date will be here in ten minutes." Money and math are one and the same. One creates a lot more interest than the other, though, so go with the money to get math principles across. Playing store is a hoot. Keep empty boxes and a calculator around. Playing store can kill half of a rainy Saturday, especially if you add the rules about being thrown out of the store if the proper store etiquette isn't followed. There is nothing more joyful as the look on a child's face as he pitches the adult from his doorstep for not saying "please." Keeping a mock checking account is also a blast. You can get all the blank checking account ledgers you want from your nearest bank. Hear your child shriek with glee as the bank teller gets to call security because they found errors on your deposit slip.

Fractions can be taught through hands-on tasks. Cut paper to specified lengths. Pretend like its expensive walnut and watch their little faces drop when they are docked a week's pay for miscutting an expensive "board". This will get you even for being handcuffed at the bank. Percentages are easy to explain if you use the criminal nature of the credit card process as an example.

You noticed that I mentioned the word "play" a lot. Play is how a child learns. There is no differentiation between work and play. Only adults separate the two. Get a child a toy vacuum cleaner or lawn mower for a present, they think it's great. Grown-ups are less cheery about it, because it signifies work, which is the adult version of a four letter word. The child's brain will absorb things quickly if they are put into a game form. And you can make a game out of anything. Instead of showing a flash card and saying "this is a five" you can have a treasure hunt for numbers and hide them around the kitchen. You can test gravity by dropping items from a high place, such as water balloons on an older brother. Science is a riot. Science is a good excuse to work on your math skills. And science is easy because science is anything you say it is.

It is Jello going from a liquid to a solid state. It is checking how many miles per gallon your family car gets and comparing it to the nitwit down the street who just bought a Sherman Tank for carrying groceries. It is a magnifying glass in a child's hand. Shoot, just buy a globe and let your child play with it. You'll be amazed how fast they can find the capital of Zimbabwe while you're still trying to locate the proper continent. And if you can't find a way to make games involving science you need to check your pulse. It may be time to give the crematorium a heads up.

During any game you are accomplishing four things: spending time with your children, which is love and bonding, having fun, imparting knowledge, and getting out of chores. "Honey, would you mow the lawn, please?" "I can't right now, because I'm playing with our precious daughter. You should see how much she is learning." This playing with the child thing is a stroke of genius. You even have a built in excuse to see every child movie ever made. There is no downside to playing. So, why are some schools set up like misery factories that kids trudge off to everyday? You need to write your local legislator and ask, because I don't have a clue. But it doesn't have to be like that in your house.

Keep in mind two things. One, is that the brain absorbs information easily and naturally. That is what it does, just as the stomach digests food. The other is that ANYTHING can be ruined if forced. A child learns to master language all by himself. If you decide to force the issue, shrieking "Not dadda, ... DADDY, DADDY," at him, you can create all kinds of speech problems not to mention the lifelong fear of DADDY. I've seen all kinds of eating disorders created by harsh, mean commands at the dinner table. Sex itself can be ruined if it is unpleasant. I've seen kids grow up hating to read or hating science. How is that even possible? It's like hating to talk. If you say things like "I said E, not E flat—E! What's the matter with you?" I can guarantee you that that child is not going to race upstairs to practice his violin during his spare time. Now, he may offer it up if a little more kindling is needed for the campfire.

So make your house a safe, fun place to learn, which leads to one last word on games. I DON'T mean competition where you have winners and losers. I mean setting up learning in a non-work atmosphere. You don't want to be prancing around the room like Mohammed Ali after beating your child in a number game while he is wailing inconsolably in the bathroom. Each child's competition lust is different and arrives at different stages in life. Let them dictate any competition. In small children, the possibility of LOSING at something often negates any possible fun and short-circuits the learning because the child is focused on not being publicly humiliated. Have fun without it. There is no such thing as a loser in learning. If you must compete have it be you and your child against a goal, or the child striving to beat his own standard.

We need to talk about the effects of TV on your child's brain sometime, and now seems as good a time as any. The power of learning through play is that the child is interacting with his environment. He is touching, smelling, tasting. Better yet, he might be interacting with other people. It is through the physical interaction with their environment that a young child learns.

The actual process of watching TV is the exact opposite of the learning process. Instead of being active, you are passive and the only environment you come into contact with is the couch. And you can't interact with people because you are constantly telling them to shut up and stop interrupting your show. I don't care how high the quality of the show is, the act of watching television is anti-learning. See this chart here? This is an eye opener. If you will notice, this rising line here, which represents hours of watching TV per day, correlates perfectly with this descending line here, which is a child's shrinking grade point average. It doesn't get any plainer than that. When you watch TV, within minutes your brainwaves go from an active pattern to something between hypnosis and sleep. Some people call television the electronic fireplace. Before TV, people used to stare at fires, which is also hypnotic. Now, if you've had a hard day at work and feel the need to come home and be entertained, which in the case of TV is hypnosis with a theme, there is absolutely nothing wrong with that. Join the club. It's a big one. But the effects on children, who should be DOING SOMETHING instead of just sitting there staring, are devastating. Why would a parent plunk their child down in front of the zombie machine for hours, everyday? Because they're wicked? Sick? Twisted? How about just plain tired? Or wore out? They need a break from real life, which is work and parenting. . . . . Oh, I see. Well, the reason why you're not worn out is that you don't have any children yet. I can give a seventeen year old powerhouse a set of twins and come back six weeks later and he's been replaced by a tired, stooped, eighty year old man with a cranky disposition. Shoot, the reason why I'm here giving you this lecture is that I'm TRYING TO SAVE YOUR LIFE. At least life as you know it now. The fact is that many adults are too tired for their own children. We ALL have to guard against the natural tendency to use the television as a babysitter. Set up some rules about TV, made before you are too tired to think, or it will rule your house. It will swallow your child whole. I have visited many households of families whose children are struggling in school. I have seen households where the TV is on all day long. All night long. Multiple TV's. There isn't a place in the house where you could have a normal conversation, much less a quiet space to have a real thought. A child should not watch much TV or computer screens at all before the age of four. After that, limit viewing to an hour or two per day, if, behaviorally and scholastically, they have earned it. Make sure that they are getting enough of what they really need, such as play, exploration, reading, conversation, etc. A little TV watching is not going to hurt anybody. The code word is "little," which means DO NOT buy a TV for your child's bedroom. I am going to jump ahead real quick to parent discipline skills. Everybody, together. Say NO! Nyet! Nein! Non! Nadda! And the old stand by, Are you kidding me? Very good. Remember that, because it will also come in very handy when you are deciding, with your child, what shows they are actually allowed to watch.

You think the act of watching television is bad, what about the content? I had a kindergarten class once. It was St. Patrick's Day, so I figured that making a leprechaun would be a fitting project. When I mentioned it to the children, however, they reacted with horror and revulsion. It took me a couple of minutes to realize that some enterprising young studio executive had recently made a movie about a diabolical, murderous leprechaun and of course, EVERY ONE of these five year olds had seen it, and now screech at the sight of anything Irish. If they can make a few more classics about murdering Santas and Easter Bunnies we can wipe out a lot of holidays, which would be a great stress reducer for adults. If you want to start a heated argument, go into your average second grade and ask who's badder, Freddy or Jason? Oh, you'll touch off something there, because they will all have an opinion, because they WILL ALL HAVE SEEN IT. Two thoughts spring immediately to mind. Where are the parents and why haven't they been kneecapped yet? Does anybody actually think that there is some kind of special soap or scrub brush out there that will erase horrible images from a child's mind? I even had a parent tell me one time that her eight year old wasn't effected by violent murder scenes. She said, no, it doesn't bother him, he just laughs at it. Now, let THAT sink in for a moment. Like, laughing while somebody is being stabbed to death is a superior response than crying and running, which is what normal people would do. Now, it is hard to talk to clueless parents, because they get very oversensitive about their ignorance, so it needs to be handled delicately. The technique that works for me is yelling, "WHAT WERE YOU THINKING ABOUT?" at them while speed dialing 911. I mean, come on now. I can see the family sitting around, looking at the movie guide. "Let's see now, we can watch "Little Fluffy Finds a Home," "Brave Jeremy Saves an Entire Family," or "Sara Goes on a Blood Soaked Killing Spree." Well, that's a no brainer. Click. "Boy, that Sara sure is something, isn't she?" I mean, really. What ARE they thinking about? I am sure that the verb "thinking" does not apply here. They are adults going through the motions of the day, surviving until the next day. I am not sure that a lot of adults appreciate the true beauty of a child, which is their sensitivity. I learned a large, unpleasant lesson once while watching TV with my daughter when she was seven. We were watching the Andy Griffith Show, which to me was a very safe, high quality show. Nothing to worry about here. Otis comes in drunk to lock himself in the cell, which is the gag. I was laughing away, even though I'd seen the episode probably two hundred times, when I noticed that my daughter not only wasn't laughing, but had a disturbed look on her face. "What is that man doing?" she asked. Well, he's drunk and . . . ." "What is drunk?" "Well, it's when somebody has had too much alcohol to drink and they get dizzy." "Why are you laughing, Daddy? I don't get it." All of a sudden I wasn't laughing anymore; in fact was feeling quite uncomfortable. I had seen this show over and over, but it had been a long, long time since I had seen it through a child's eyes. Explaining alcohol abuse as humor is impossible. The more I tried, the more uncomfortable I got and the more confused she got. I switched to the Muppets Show and just prayed that there were no wine jokes in it. As adults, we often forget how sensitive kids are, because we've seen and done way too much. That television experience with my daughter was a wake-up call. If children can discern disturbing elements in even the most innocent settings, what does viewing full throttle violence do to their minds? I suggest that you don't beat their sensitivity into callousness and indifference by pounding them with negative images. You are literally pounding the childhood right out of them.

I am going to press three points here, all interrelated: the power of images, the role of violence in brain development, and the formation of a child's own self image. Images, once seen, can never be erased from the brain. Never. The brain may try its best to sublimate, or bury, certain unpleasant images, but they are still there. They can still be seen decades later. We have all seen unpleasant things. Conjure one up. See? They're still there. At my age I can still remember my younger brother getting sick all over the inside of my dad's car. Of course, that happened just last week, so I guess that doesn't count. As a parent, you have a responsibility and a duty to let your child be a child by shielding them from things that they should not see. I am talking mostly about violence and sex. There is absolutely no excuse for exposing your children to this. None. There are laws against it which are never enforced, but it is nevertheless criminal, because the effects are everlasting and serious. There have been several studies done on violence and children. A child immersed in violence has a brain that attends to information differently from one that isn't. Some kids stare at the blackboard to glean information, while others stare worriedly over their right shoulder to keep an eye on behavioral challenged classmates. If you find yourself living in a violent community it is especially important that you pull "Fluffy Finds a Home" off the shelf, because there has to be a mental safe harbor somewhere. Which child do you want to have in school? The one who is studiously caring for his plant in the science fair, experimenting on how the chlorophyll process can be adapted somehow for the betterment of mankind, or Jimmy The Thug, who is concentrating on how many of his boys he can talk into jumping on the young scientist who had accidentally brushed up against him in the hallway? Violence is the enemy. The problem with violence is that it consumes all the air in the room. I don't care what is going on, violence has the ability to take it over and destroy it. You can be at the mall, a ball game, a doctor's office, or a classroom, and if a fight breaks out all normalcy in that situation is lost. All attention goes to the violence. All activity goes to it, either by stopping it, fueling it, or avoiding it. All conversation revolves around it, even for days after. Take a long look at a nine year old. How much has violence and his reaction to it taken over his brain? Does he attend to positives, academics, and construction, or negatives, violence, and destruction? Are his conversations mostly positive or negative? When I was in high school many of my conversations revolved around a girlfriend, real or imagined. Nowadays the conversation revolves around who is going to beat whom up, real or imagined. There is a lot of violence in the world these days. Do not throw gas on the fire by showing a child lots of negative images. Remember, all a child really wants to be is an adult. What kind of adult? Normal is whatever a child is surrounded by. Hate, fighting, yelling, or love, cooperation and respect are all normal to a child that knows nothing else. You are raising an adult when you are raising a child. What you get out of it is what you put into it. Monkey see, monkey do rules the world.

What is your own image of your child? Do you want your child to be productive and stay out of jail? Then don't let him see countless images that tell him that's exactly where he's going. Where, in fact, he belongs, as if he's got some kind of sacred jail destiny. One day you will find things coming out of your mouth that will sound eerily like whatever crazy thing your parents said to you when they were mad, like, "WHO DO YOU THINK YOU ARE?" That's the anti-disrespect response. The child is steady talking back to dad, telling dad what to do and what not to do. What you are going to get is, "WHO DO THINK YOU ARE?" often followed by some kind of atomic explosion. And you know what? That is probably one of the most important questions that a parent can ask. Who DOES little Robert think he is? Everything this child does, good or bad, is related to his own self image. The power of outside images is that after awhile they get internalized. The outside becomes the inside, and once inside that child's own head and heart, what do you do? Teaching a child who thinks that he is stupid or bad is an entirely different ballgame than one who has a self view of being smart or good. If a child internalizes a negative view of himself it puts up huge barriers between him and his parents and teachers. Once that barrier is erected adults find themselves less and less trying to teach little Robert and more and more trying to save Robert from his own destructive tendencies.

What is a parent's image of their child? Some parents, and I'm one of them, firmly believe that a child can be anything he wants to be if he is willing to work hard for it. This belief is enormously important because if you believe it, the child will come to believe it. I find it to be absolutely true. A child's own belief system is going to shape their life. Like many things, this is a two edged sword. If they want to be a plumber or architect, that's fine. They may actually be helpful to you in your old age. But what if they want to be a criminal? I'll say that again. What if they REALLY think that they are going to be a criminal? What are you, as parent, going to do about it? Because they will meet their own perceived fate if you just stand there, staring in disbelief. I was mentoring a group of ninth graders once: the same group, once a week, all year long, so we had a good rapport with each other. Towards the end of the year I posed the question of how they saw themselves making money ten years into the future. The fact that most didn't even think they were going to live that long, much less PLAN for it should have been a hint that this might not go well. One at a time I wrote their ideas on the board. When it was done, we all sat back and looked at our collaboration. This is a true story, I swear it. We had written selling drugs, stealing, getting pregnant for the check, getting someone else pregnant for the check, just going to the mailbox and getting a check, winning the lottery, playing professional sports, or being a rap or music star. That's it. Period. Let me tell you something, you could hear a pin drop in that room when we were done. I wasn't shocked, but they sure were. They had never come face to face with the ugly reality that they carried around in their heads and hearts. Your own self image is something that you are not really aware of, it just slowly develops over time. It's like breathing. You don't notice it, but it's there and influences everything you do.

So who DOES your child think he is? If you cannot see the posters of rock stars dressed all in black through the curtain of skulls that your teenager has put up, you might want to have a talk with him. If your child refers to you as my maid b . . . instead of mom it may be a sign to bring out the hammer, what a parent would call a CD equalizer. If your daughter wants to wear a G-string for Halloween and go as a video background star you may want to find a couple of minutes out of your busy day to have a little chat. If your son has his underwear showing 92% of the time, this tells you exactly how that child views himself. He's probably not modeling himself after a doctor.

A positive self-image is even more important for children with learning disabilities. All people, no matter what age, want to feel powerful, which really means having control over their life. Nobody desires to be helpless, living in a world where things just happen to you. And, if you are powerless, one senses that a lot of those things aren't going to be good.

Where does power come from? Many places, which can be a bit of a problem for human beings. It can come from the head: intellect, wit, academic ability, problem solving. It can come from the heart: compassion, empathy, charity. It can come from the body: physical prowess, agility, beauty. It can come from the soul: art, drama, music. These are all positive and productive.

But what if your child struggles in school and is made fun of? What if school is a place where they feel uncomfortable, inferior, helpless, powerless? What is that child going to do? Go to the other source of power, of course. A veritable fountain of power. Go to the DARK SIDE. Money, sex, violence. The shortcuts to success. Take Suzie. She can't read very well and math to her is like learning Chinese. Every time she tries to put pen to paper, it doesn't turn out so well. More like a seven year old than a seventeen year old. But put her in a thong bikini and men—not just boys, but grown men—would happily enter a point-blank shotgun contest just to spend five minutes with her. Now, where does she view her power source? Is it more likely that Suzie will become a leading cancer researcher or a pole dancer at Big Daddy's Fun Club?

Take Steven. He is laughed at all day at school. Thought per cent was cat money. Martin Luther King, Jr. was president during the civil war. His science fair project was a stick. But at midnight he can make more money in an hour than a teacher earns in a month and just by whipping his gun out while growling like a preliterate Neanderthal can clear an entire parking lot in under five seconds. Where, exactly, does Steven think his power is coming from? Is it more likely that he will become a craftsman carpenter, or do ten to twenty at the state's Dude Ranch Gone Bad?

Students who are struggling at school, especially those with learning disabilities, are cannon fodder for people who make their money off of negative power sources. Shoot, there are millions of kids with absolutely no faith in their intellectual abilities to do anything positive. A giant army of Darth Vader wannabes marching to the thug-life drummer.

So, what is a parent to do? Get mad. Repeat after me, NOT MY CHILD . . . . Is that the best you can do? People are stealing your children. Come on gentlemen, everybody up. Now give me that power stance. You know how to do it. Give me the arms folded, head cocked, glaring thing. There you go. Now let's use it for something more useful than terrorizing your grandmother into letting you stay out late. NOT MY CHILD . . . . NOT MY CHILD.

Now, parents-to-be, we're not helpless. Let's DO something. Let's use what we know to our advantage. If a child feels the power of their intellectual ability, they are much less likely to go to the dark side for a power source. Constantly praise and nurture intellectual ability. It is easy to fall into the old habits of telling a girl how pretty she is or a boy how strong he is. There is nothing wrong with that as long as you also add what a genius you think he or she is. Also, self—image develops early, so plan on planting positive images from birth. How you and your spouse conduct each other are the first images your child will internalize. Images are powerful. Use that power by being a positive role model and surround your child with pictures of positive role models. If your child is an Hispanic girl named Maria, some of the pictures in her house should be of Hispanic women doing positive things: doctor, pilot, scientist, brick mason. You don't have to lecture Maria in her crib about how all things are possible, because she will have grown up seeing it. When it becomes internalized, seeing it becomes believing it.

If you believe that something is possible, then in reality it becomes possible. Case in point: a famous black actor—I believe it was Will Smith, but my memory isn't what it once was-said that when he was young, seeing Ohura sitting at her station on the starship Enterprise while he was watching Star Trek opened all kinds of mental doors for him. Black people in positions of importance, as scientists, as ACTORS. Once the mental door is opened it just becomes a matter of motivation to walk through it.

One of the best positive imaging posters of all time is next on this chart. This is from World War II. Women were desperately needed to work in munitions factories and other "male" jobs. Here is Rosie the Riveter, a woman showing her toughness in a typically male pose, flexing her muscles, with the words WE CAN DO IT emblazoned on it. How powerful is that? How many millions of girls and boys had their world view changed because of that image? How many millions of mental doors did this open up, especially at a time when, normally, if a poster were made with women in it, they would be standing in the middle of a kitchen?

The story of the four minute mile is illuminating. For years running a four minute mile was thought impossible. Not just real hard, but impossible. Until somebody broke it. Not too long after that the record was broken again, several times, because the mental block about it being impossible was gone. People had SEEN it beaten.

So put any kind of barrier busting pictures on the wall you want. They will open a floodgate of mental possibilities for your child. Black Nobel Prize winning scientists, female heavy equipment operators, male nurses, Chinese cowboys, the famous Jamaican bobsledders. And if you're putting pictures on the wall for boys, make sure most of the men are smiling. And gunless. I mean, what is up with the images of young men these days? Everybody has to be tough. This macho hate-stare thing has got to go. Like it's against the law to be friendly. As if that's anti-man. This is why so many kids carry weapons. If a man is supposed to be hard, as tough as a brick, with the emotional feelings of a toaster, then carrying a gun makes sense. It makes you an instant man, without having to go through all the mental gymnastics of things that make an adult's head hurt, like telling the difference between right and wrong. So put some HAPPY people on the wall. Lot's of them. "Gee, I don't know why my child has such a negative view of life." Well, if manhood has been defined by negative images, what do you expect? And ladies, you can help here, you know, by not encouraging the modern hate man. If you are attracted by the fact that your boyfriend can't hold a job and is only seconds away from becoming violently unhinged, you need to give Oprah or Phil a call and talk this thing out. And stop dancing to songs that call you disgraceful things. I mean, if the band was joyfully playing "You're a four eyed white trash idiot" I don't think you'd find me on the dance floor doing the Glide.

Which leads me to audio imaging. What you hear is almost as important as what you see and all of the same rules apply. Keep what a child hears positive in nature. A young teacher at a faculty meeting once said, "You know, it's not Aretha Franklin any more. It's kill, kill, murder, murder." What an eloquent observation. Listen to some Motown from the sixties. The Supreme's "Stop In The Name Of Love" would now be "Stop, You B . . . . Before I Snap Your Collarbone."

Control, for as long as you can, what your child hears. The ears are a direct conduit to the brain, which is what we are trying to build up. If your four year old is exposed to constant cursing don't be shocked when "Grandpa" becomes "That blankety blank old blank."

When I say control what a child hears, I am not just talking about hovering over the CD player. What, as a PARENT, you say to your child carries more weight than what anybody on the planet can say. So, for heaven's sake, don't EVER call your child stupid or any other adjective that implies stupid. I don't care what kind of stupid thing that child has done. You can find him in the middle of your beloved flower garden munching on your Zinnias while he is burying your only car key and you still can't impugn his brain capacity, because he will internalize it. It will become his world view. If you call your child a mean, disrespectful, lazy imbecile, be prepared for the phone call from school saying that your little Shirley flunked her test, slept through class, cursed the teacher when she woke her, and beat up Shonterrica because she was looking at her the wrong way. You shake your head sadly. "I just don't know what got into her." What do you mean you don't know what got into her? YOU got into her.

So you've got to find a positive way of addressing a child when they mess up. I suggest practice BEFORE a child messes up, because it's hard to do when you are furious and yelling. I'm going to talk about discipline, per se, in a minute, but this is it's foundation: It's not the child you are mad at, but the ridiculous BEHAVIOR that he is exhibiting. This is so important that it is not just rule number one, but actually rule one through twenty. If the parent internalizes this, then positive discipline becomes much easier. Basically, you're not mad at your youngster, but at the fact that he has somehow now learned how to spell misdemeanor. If a child feels that you love them and you have their best interest at heart, they will accept any reasonable discipline you mete out. If a child feels that you hate them, then it becomes a battle of whether or not you have the ability to make them obey. A child is going to respond to where they think that discipline is coming from. Always lead with a positive, self-image building statement, THEN put the hammer down.

An example: I used to work at a last chance type of facility that kids were sent to for zero tolerance offenses, usually fighting or drugs. Sometimes fighting over the drugs, while on the drugs. They're basically good kids with a very limited and violent set of tools to deal with life. Occasionally I'd get a call in my office from a teacher telling me that a student was out of control in their class. Since my job title was Mr. Control, I would go to the room and remove the student so the teacher could perform his job title. Let's say I'm dealing with Franco, who weighs 220 lbs. and is sixteen years old. The very first thing that comes out of my mouth when I enter the room is "Now, Franco, you know I love you. Love you all day long. And I have all the faith in the world that you are going to become the highly paid and highly qualified auto mechanic that you are striving to become because you are a genius with cars, but writing profanity on Sherita's backside with her own eye liner is unacceptable. Come with me, please." They would always come with no further trouble. Why? I did not attack them, so there was nothing to defend. I told the child one, I love them, two, that everything I do is to ensure a brighter future, that I believe they HAVE a brighter future, and finally, that I will punish, if need be, to ensure that bright future. And I have set the stage, in a positive way, for any escalation of force that is needed. Children will accept any and all discipline if it comes from a positive place.

How is Franco's self image after all this? Absolutely intact. During this uproar he has been loved and called competent to the point of genius. That's exactly what I want, because if he believes that about himself he will react accordingly during the punishment phase. What I'll get is, "I'm sorry. I know I can do better. I promise." And he will, in fact, do so.

Gentlemen, does a grown man saying, "I love you" to a male teenager seem a little strange to you? Sure it does. And that's too bad. It seems strange because, first of all, you think love means sex, which it doesn't because they are two completely different things. And second of all, many males don't have fathers so they have never heard it in their entire life.

You know the reaction I would get when I walk into a room and say "You know I love you but" . . . . ? At first, of course, laughter and disbelief. After awhile, however, when I'd enter the room to deal with a situation, I'd be greeted with a chorus of "We love you Mr. Johnson." I'd follow with, "Ah, yes, I'm full of love today. It's a beautiful day. Now Johnny, untie Mr. Jefferson, please. And give me the sword before you hurt somebody."

Males of all ages are literally dying to hear, "I love you" coming from a father figure. They are beating and stabbing and shooting and hating each other because no man in their life has taken the time to show them that being a man is love, not hardness, coldness, toughness, meanness, hate. Gentlemen, I am going to repeat this one more time. DO NOT RUN OUT ON YOUR CHILDREN. YOU ARE MORE IMPORTANT THAN YOU THINK.

To review: positive self-image is, one, lead with I love you but . . . . , you are a genius but . . . . or whatever positive phrase you want. Two, tie to destiny self-image. "You're going to be a great dress designer someday, but . . . . ," then the discipline that seems appropriate.

One last word on building a positive self-image in your child. Empty praise will not get you there. "Oh, Brandon, that was great. You are so smart. Daddy is so proud of you." DON'T say all of this when all the child has done is sneezed all over himself. You can say I love you all day long, but save the praise for when they've actually done something. Praise the accomplishment. "Brandon, you mowed the entire lawn and left the rose bushes intact this time. Great job." Or, "Barbara, you've memorized all of your times tables. That's very smart, girl. Now we can apply it to your trigonometry homework."

By praising accomplishments, or good efforts towards a goal, the child's positive self-image that she is building will stand the child in good stead later on in life when it gets tough because it was based on reality. The child is developing faith in her own mental and physical abilities to reach a goal. This is hugely important. If child "A" has a goal of earning a good income and faith in his own abilities to do so, he may spend his time steering towards his goal through studies and hard work. If child "B" has the same goal, but no faith in his abilities to achieve it, he will spend his time stalking child "A". Ability based praise will build an adult who is confident and competent. Empty praise, just to make the child feel good, will build a swelled head and a sense of entitlement much like a spoiled rotten prince who demands to take a pony from another child simply because he is the king's son. Or the CEO who thinks he deserves a 200 million dollar severance package even though the company is going into the dump.

Faith in ability will get a child through hard as well as good times. Faith in entitlement only works if everything is flowing your way, like being lucky enough to be born to the king instead of the hot, sweaty blacksmith down the street, who actually works for a living. How can you tell what kind of child you've got? Ask them what they want to do in life. If they reply lay on the couch all day, and mean it, you have a large, expensive entitlement problem on your hands.

And don't think for one second that you're fooling the kid with your empty praise. When I was in junior high school I could be told all day long by well meaning adults about how great a dancer I was, but I knew in reality I was going to make a big, fat fool out of myself the very second I hit the dance floor. I knew my ability level, as all children do, so I would spend dance night terrified and sick. "Oh, Martha, what an exquisite piece of art. It's beautiful. And at your age." "Mom, it's a purple line. My hand slipped. And I just turned twenty-six." So, please stick with ability, effort, and success based praise.

I'm going to touch on routines for a moment. So far we've laid an excellent foundation for raising a success oriented child. It will help greatly if you stick to certain routines each day, such as bed time, meal time, reading time, and play time with you. At first glance children seem to like chaos. A close reading of "The Lord of the Flies" shows that kids may gravitate to chaos, but not necessarily like it.

Children's brains are constantly trying to create order in the middle of disorder. Give a group of children some toys and tell them to play, with no other instructions than to just have fun. What are the kids going to do? Spend two hours arguing over the rules. Guaranteed. If you have routines that are consistent, it frees the child's mind up for other things besides trying to create order, such as thinking, learning and creating. If you don't have any consistency in the house the child's mind will be constantly testing and probing where some boundaries are and the thinking and learning thing will take a back seat. Case in point. Larry is going home from school, as he always does at four o'clock. He runs to the house to be greeted by mom, as always. Except this time mom is not there. No note. Just not there. It's an empty house. Now, what is Larry going to do? Is he going to meticulously lay out all of his homework, books, pencils and get to work so that he is done by dinner? Or is he going to rip his hair out as he runs frantically from room to room searching for his mother, because she may have run off with a motorcycle gang and is right now driving wildly through the mountains of North Carolina, like she's been threatening to do for the last ten years.

There is not a child on this planet that would sit down and do his homework under those circumstances. What if it happens a lot? What if mom and dad are missing a lot and the child doesn't know where they are? What do you think that child is thinking about at school? Geometry? What if some days there is food and other days not? What if sometimes he goes to bed at nine o'clock and other times at

one o'clock in the morning? What if sometimes dad is sweet and playful and other times violent and moody?

Consistency is very important for a child's learning ability and routines are a way for that consistency to be formalized in your house. Consistency is the cornerstone for learning. All science and math are based on it. How could the adult mind function if gravity was just an occasional thing? Sometimes hot air rises and sometimes it falls? Have a carpool bet each morning on which direction the sun will rise from?

The human brain is an ordering, organizing machine. If there was no sense to the universe, if everything was random, the brain would go mad spending all it's time trying to create some semblance of order. If there is no order in your house, which is the child's universe, their brain will spend most of it's energy trying to figure out WHAT in the heck is going on.

The only thing your child is going to learn is the fine art of arguing. And not the logic based type of arguing that might do her some good when she is a lawyer. No, no. We're talking chaos based arguing here. "Why do I have to go to bed now? You let me watch the "Late, Late Show" last night. Why do I have to read today? I got to watch TV all last year. You didn't say anything then. What do you mean I can't drink beer today? You let me last Tuesday. So, what, Tuesday is beer day or something? Let me know when it's crack day. That's the one I don't want to miss." Consistency is all the more important in your home, because the school that your child is going to attend could be Anarchy High, named after the children who didn't get any structure at their home. And if they don't get structure at home or at school, they'll probably end up at Structure University, which is prison. The voluntary one is the military.

One routine I'd like to emphasize is bedtime. Plenty of sleep is important for children. Not only is this when the body repairs itself, but the brain processes the day's information, also. Memory and information retrieval paths are being worked on as well as all of the emotional drama of the day. If your child is punching the pillow in his sleep while yelling, "I hate algebra, but mostly I hate you, Mrs. Davis," don't worry. It's perfectly normal. It's just a reminder to call the school early the next morning.

This memory consolidation thing is kind of important. It helps not just in real life, but in school too. "Mrs. Klein, your son can't remember half of his spelling words or any of his times tables. Does he get enough sleep at night?" "Well, let me see. He did get in a couple of hours last Thursday. We've been celebrating Octoberfest recently." "Mrs. Klein, it's April 5th. Why don't we give it a rest for a little bit?" I have a word of advice. If you don't want your child to learn anything, don't send him to school in the first place. Just stay up all night playing cards in the attic, where the authorities can't find you. Even if the authorities do find your child you won't get into any trouble. He won't be able to remember his OR your name. You're in the clear.

PLEASE establish a good bedtime. The bedtime routine is great, because a lot of other routines can be built around it. Reading a book out loud, recapping the day, prayer and giving thanks, if that is what your religion dictates. I realize that some religions dictate blowing up the bed, but in most households reading, conversation and prayers seem to suffice.

We are getting near to the end of our time here. Let's see what we've got. We've got a healthy child with a strong emotional and intellectual foundation for success in life, because you've followed the plan that you've set forth for her upbringing. A good, solid, adult plan. The problem is, the child hates the adult plan because it clashes with the child's plan, which is to do anything he or she wants, whenever they want to do it. The child doesn't want the adult plan because he's obviously not intent on living long enough to actually be an adult. It is up to you to make sure that they live until their 18th birthday. If they die an unnatural death before 18, it's on you. After 18, it's their bad.

How in the world are you going to execute your well thought out success plan when every facet of our society, everywhere you turn, is trying to tell your child to do the exact opposite? And he, of course, agrees with them.

Because you are the child's PARENTS. Not friend, neighbor, cousin, acquaintance, roommate or homey. The ROLE of parent is unique. It means, by the laws of nature, that you are IN CHARGE. Now, like all businesses, if you don't want to be the boss, then don't apply for the job, because you will find a horde of employees who are depending on you for their livelihood staring anxiously at you, waiting to see what to do next. If shrugging your shoulders or hiding in the alley so they don't see you cry are the two best options that you can come up with, it is a sign that you are not boss material.

But if you have come to the stage of life where you feel the competence to actually be the boss, be the parent, then do so, because children do not raise themselves. Raise is a verb, which means that a parent has to actually do something, which is why you carry your success parenting plan in your back pocket, where it is handy.

This "in charge" deal needs to be established, however. The child isn't born knowing who's in charge. In fact, he is born thinking that he is in charge. Of everything. Is, in fact, the center of the entire universe. And a bright kid with an interest in physics will tell you that he is the center of all the parallel universes also.

Besides safety, the single most important thing that a parent can do is establish the RIGHT OF LEGITIMATE AUTHORITY in the child's mind. Early. The first thing you do is take the infant over to a celestial map and point out that, not only is he not the center of the universe, but not even the center of his own little solar system. This little tidbit of information will not be welcomed, as Galileo and a host of jailed and beaten mathematicians were to find out in earlier times. You, as a parent, have a distinct advantage over Galileo, however. You are bigger than your adversary. Use the advantage now, because it won't always be that way. You are also smarter. For now. Don't let the moment slip away.

What is legitimate authority? The fact that, as a child, and later as an adult, we mutually agree as a society that there are times that we have to do as we are told, even if we don't like it. And that there are certain roles that we play as adults that give us the right to tell others what to do. And if we abide by these roles, we can enjoy the fruits of what is called civilization, as opposed to life in a mosh pit.

Decree number one is that a child MUST listen to his parents. Period. Debate is over. Debate never even began. If you can't enforce decree number one, then burn all of your other decrees because your empire will crumble to dust as the Vandals and Huns have a picnic in downtown Rome.

This is not being mean. It's not being unfair. This is simply the way it works. And it's for the child's own good because, unbeknownst to him, his very survival depends on this parent-child relationship. And, really, there is no other way that it can work. Even a child knows that. Even a child who has lost her mind knows that. I was in a student-parent meeting once and the fourteen year old student started cursing at her mother. I pulled her aside, literally, and asked her if she would allow her own child to talk to her like that. She looked at me like I was crazy. "No child of mine is going to curse me. They are going to RESPECT me."

R..E..S..P..E..C..T. Respect is how we acknowledge legitimate authority. It is the glue that holds society together. It is a courteous nod to the ROLE: parent, teacher, police officer, firefighter, etc. When the child was cursing her mother she wasn't just showing her contempt for Sally, the person, but for the role of mother itself. And if the ROLE of mother is disrespected, as in "I don't have to listen to my mother," which translates into "I don't have to listen to anybody on this planet," which really means, "Can somebody whom I haven't offended yet please send me bail money?"

So, how does a child, who clearly knows better, end up cursing out her mother? Because she can. It has never been established IN HER MIND that what she is doing is unacceptable. One of the casualties of never learning respect is having no self-respect.

The question now is, how do you get respect for legitimate authority into a child's mind? You start from infancy. You make it a natural rule of law. There is gravity, electro-magnetic forces, laws of inertia and parents are in charge of the family and are to be respected. The child will accept all this as normal, which frees his mind up to go about the business of being a child. If this parent-child role isn't established then your child thinks that he is a co-equal adult. Co-equal if you're lucky. You will have a tiny, immature but forceful adult to argue with about anything. You don't EVER want your child to think that they are your equal, unless your idea of a good conversation is begging and pleading. And I mean coming from you. You might as well invite a midget version of Genghis Khan to move in with you. Tyrant comes from the Latin word meaning toddler.

And you better establish this child-parent relationship early. You don't want to wait until they're sixteen and interrupt them while they're cleaning their AK-47 to have a talk about who's boss in the house. Besides, if you don't establish who's boss early, you can't ever use the parent's short but brilliantly effective motivational tool, which is,

"Because I said so." The only way that works is if the word "I", meaning parent, actually stands for something. If the child views you as Timmy The Big Turnip, then "Because I said so" doesn't carry much weight. There is nothing wrong with discussing or even negotiating a decision with your child. But negotiating after the decision has been made is called surrender. An ill-tempered buck private is now running your household because the general abdicated his authority.

When giving a command, you don't want a child thinking that now it's time for them to weigh their options. "Let's see, should I run blindly out into the street risking instant death or paralysis OR should I go to mommy who is, as I ponder, yelling at me to get back from the curb. What to do, what to do?" How about DO AS YOU'RE TOLD? This is not congress, where you get to debate endlessly and then do nothing. This is real life here. The small child debating society holds it's meetings in hospitals, because that's where most of its members reside. The ones in the cemetery didn't make the debate team . . . . What's that? I'm ruining your Saturday? Well, yes, I guess the death of a child will do that. Probably put a damper on Sunday through Friday, also. That's precisely why we are spending this wonderful quality time together today. If there is no parent role to say no and have it obeyed, bad junk happens. Cemetery, hospital, courthouse, prison: these are the playgrounds for children who feel they don't have to listen to anybody, and not one of those places has the word university attached to it . . . . You look upset, sweetheart. Sex is a strange business. It has a lot of baggage that goes with it: emotionally, physically, spiritually. It has all of these side avenues that you don't even think about when you're fifteen. As a parent, you have to think about unpleasant things, though. You don't have the luxury of ignoring the consequences, of pretending, which is child-think. What, exactly, do you suppose a small child is going to do when your back is turned for even one second? The very SECOND you're not looking that child is going to go explore his world, which translates into, "Martha, you better run get your boy because it looks like he's trying to kill himself." You don't know what they're going to do, except that it involves bodily harm. Now, you can have a child when you're fifteen if you want to, but when your hair turns shock white when you're seventeen, I don't want to hear about it . . . . I see. You thought that parents bossing you around

42

was just because they want to micro-manage your life, as if they didn't have enough to do. I am sure it seems that way sometimes. It's all about their intense fear of losing someone as precious as you. Little Luellen: "I hope she doesn't fall and hurt herself." Big Luellen out on a date: "I hope she gets home on time and doesn't die in a flaming car wreck." It'll be that way, no matter what your age. If you are old and in a walker and your mother is still alive, it'll be like the old days. She'll be worried about you falling and hurting yourself again. It is in the nature of the relationship. What you don't want is, "Where's Luellen?" "I don't know, who cares?"

To recap: you have GOT to establish parental authority in your house for the safety and welfare of the child. O.K., Mr. Authority, all dressed up in your fancy authority uniform, feeling powerful, lord of the house and lawn, Mr. Because I Said So: you have just asked your child to do something and they look up at you with that adoring, cute little face and respond with, "NO!" Don't look shocked. The child still loves you. It's just what we in the education field call a teachable moment. If your child has never said a defiant "NO" to you it's because you've never asked them to do anything besides eat ice cream and watch television. Now, there are many ways for a general to deal with open rebellion. There are whole books written on the subject. Pick one off the shelf and use it, because if the rebellion succeeds the coup de tat is over and you are now looking at a life of perpetual k-p duty and walking the perimeter. I am going to tell you a true story. I was outside in my yard, which I earned by working for a living. I asked my son to pick up some sticks and put them in the wheelbarrow so that I could mow the lawn safely. He's a little surly because he'd rather be inside watching TV, so I decided to make a game out of it, which I often try to do with chores. I started throwing sticks in from different parts of the yard. I began to notice that I was the only one working on my jump shot, however, so I again asked him to help. He said that he didn't feel like it because his back hurt. Two things ran through my mind at the same time. One, was the fact that his back didn't seem to hurt much when he was doing flips in the air conditioned living room and two, was that he didn't seem overly concerned about the fact that I had a long week and maybe my back was bothering me, too. I asked him ever so politely, but he said a little more firmly, "I don't feel like it." The yard was no longer my focal point. "Son, this work needs to be done and I need your help." "Why do I have to bend over and pick up sticks? They're not really bothering anything." "Because I'm your father and I said so. Start over there and put them in the cart, NOW." I've gone from asking to telling. That's when it came rolling out. "NO!" It probably surprised him as much as me. He had never flat out said "NO" before. So there it was, for all the world to see. I measured my words carefully. "Son, you are a great kid and I love you, but you are going to pick up these sticks. If I have to spank you to do so, so be it. It's your choice. Are you going to fill that wheelbarrow, or not?" He was a good kid and like all kids had been punished before, by time-outs, no TV or loss of privileges, but he had never been spanked before because he had never put himself in the position to be spanked, which, to me, is showing open defiance. We eyeballed each other a little more but evidently the mere threat of a spanking didn't do it. He had made up his mind. "NO!" The spanking itself lasted two seconds at most and wasn't particularly painful, but the effect was electric. I had a yard to be proud of and, after the weeping and sobbing was over, one in which I could enjoy time with my family. And my family was intact again. Each person, parent and child, was back firmly in their proper role. You know what my son said later on that day? . . . . No, he didn't curse me. He said, "I'm sorry dad." This implied several things, including the knowledge that he was wrong and didn't blame me for correcting the situation. I told him that I loved him and was sorry that I had to do what I had to do. We laughed at the basic stupidity of the whole incident and went on about our day. As an aside, if a loving parent-child relationship is established from birth and positive discipline tools are used, the resort to a spanking will almost never happen.

I had an enlightening moment at an Academy once. We had a girl, who I will call Suzie, go ballistic, trying to kick out the windows and doors of the office and assault everybody in an attempt to run away. While the police were taking the young lady away in handcuffs and putting her into the back seat of the police car, an adult volunteer at the school looked at me and said, "You know, there's something terribly wrong here. Society is willing to put this girl in jail, but think it's wrong to spank her to prevent it." No truer words have ever been spoken. I am NOT advocating spanking, per se, but there must be a fair but severe punishment designed for open rebellion. Saving the family unit is that important. This girl had always run her household and as she got older it got less and less funny. Unless something is done she will end up trying to rule over a bunch of girls just like her. Being boss in a prison is not quite as easy as whipping up on a ninety pound aunt or throwing grandma down a flight of stairs. Every member of a family should have to sign a contract stipulating that, no matter what they do, it will not involve destroying the family unit because, in reality, that's all that most of us have that stands between a decent standard of living and living in a tin lean-to and eating on the soup line. Nobody is allowed to step out of their assigned role. The child cannot be the adult, as we've seen, and the adult cannot be the child, which happens a lot also. "Dad, where are you going?" "To the strip club." "But Dad, it's a school night. How about a little help here?" A lot of this mess is not of Suzie's own making. Her family was so dysfunctional that she never learned what a child's place is in the family, or really what a family is besides a collection of relatives in a house. Being a head of a family, with all it's complexities, is like driving a speeding train. In this particular family, they let tiny Casey Jones climb into the cab and be the engineer. We all know how that turned out. The worst part about tiny Casey Jones is that she is like Jason: she never dies. Just walks away from the train wreck and jumps aboard another train. If the family is destroyed, what next? Casey sees the train marked "school" and scrambles on board that one. Not in the rear, of course. She heads straight for the engineer's seat.

As a teacher, you can tell the students a mile away who run their own homes. When they enter school they full well expect to run the classroom, and don't mind who knows it. And if you ask them to do something that they don't feel like doing, they'll turn all lawyer on you. "I know my rights." Let me give you the reasoned response of Thomas Jefferson, author of the Declaration of Independence and one of the founders of the concept of the public school system. And I quote: "Have you lost your mind? Have you been drinking before school again? Sit down and do your work, please. You do have rights, but not the "I'm going to run the class" kind. You are an adult in training, which is called a child. Don't make me show you what I did to the British." "I know my rights." Don't make me laugh. And if you don't establish the parent-child relationship early, that's all any adult is ever going to hear from your kid: "I know my rights."

"Why do the Asians do so well in school?" I heard a mother pondering this while she was waiting for her child to come out of the principal's office. "I don't understand how, out of a student body of 1,500 people, only two of whom are Asian, both of them were tied for class valedictorian." Well, Kim Wong didn't spend one second of her time trying to figure out who the teacher was in the class, her or the older person. She put all her energies into her studies. When she boarded the train, she didn't run to the cab to hijack it. She got into the passenger car with her laptop. By the time Casey Jones had her wreck, Kim was putting the finishing touches on a new aero-dynamic design so that the train would run more efficiently.

The whole point here is that discipline is good for the child as well as for the family and society. Essential for the child because it takes a lot of the foolishness out of the ball game so that the child can focus their energies on positive things. As a teacher, the number two phrase that you are likely to hear after making a request of a student, right after "I know my rights" is "You're not my daddy." What a breath taking statement this is. And what a revealing one. There is no further proof needed of the damage done to a child when there is no father present in their life than the bitter shouting of, "You're not my daddy!" when asked to do something by an authority figure. For a teacher it is an invaluable statement because it tells volumes about the child. Ninety-nine out of a hundred times it tells me that the child has no father. And they aren't too happy about it. And they're so hacked off about being abandoned that they aren't going to let you or any other do-gooder adult fill the role because, as has been forcefully and eloquently stated, "You're not my daddy." It's when they erupt with, "You're not my daddy," or it's cousin, "You can't make me," that the extent of the damage becomes clear. Children usually go through the "You can't make me" stage around two years old. The official medical term for this stage is the terrible twos. Another something for you would-be parents to look forward to. The stage ends when they are actually MADE to do something, which usually involves a lot of crying, kicking and screaming. Once the child realizes he is not the CEO of the company, but a stockroom clerk instead, life returns to normal. If there is no authority figure in the house it is virtually impossible for the child to ever have a normal life. You have got a two year old stuck in a sixteen year old body. Just a heads up here. I have no idea how the dating thing works anymore, but I have a feeling that most teenagers of the opposite sex are not turned on by infants. Let me tell you two real life stories.

I had a parent-teacher conference once with a teenaged boy being raised by his grandmother. She said to me, "Mr. Johnson, I think you're being too hard on Kevin. You should do what I do when he gets really angry. I lock myself in the bathroom and after a couple of hours he calms down." The principal explained to her that our classrooms weren't equipped with bathrooms to hide in, so that wasn't an option. She was very understanding. Now, bless her heart, she was doing the best that she could. But her best wasn't helping her grandson any. Later in the year I ended up taking a gun and bullets from the young man. I still have the bullets in my den. That poor woman should never have been in this position. Where was the rest of the family unit?

I had another young man, around sixteen years old, who would start every class with a defiant, "You can't make me read." Think about that one for a moment. What a profound window into his world view. That's his entire life. "You can't make me eat." Yeah, O.K. You've got a point. Unfortunately, this sets young adults up for the "Yes, we can make you" hotel, which is jail. And the juvenile justice system in the United States is so ineffective, that it isn't until the clang of a prison cell reverberates in their ears that their "You can't make me" world actually crumbles. What a waste of a life. This is why proper parenting is so important and why I am spending my Saturday here doing my best to drive you crazy.

Now, I myself am crazier than most teachers and took the "you can't make me read" as a personal challenge. I, in fact MADE him read. It was a daily adventure into the world of professional wrestling. Ten years later he returned to say hello. He was dressed in his full military uniform. He said that because he could read he got to ride in the tank instead of being relegated to menial duties, such as washing the tank. This is the entire reason for good parenting. I have said this before but it's worth repeating. EVERY child has a success destiny. It is up to the parent to instill the skills and set the foundation for that success. Which brings me to the phrase "tough love." Since your generation is eaten up with the desire for tattoos and is rushing headlong to have babies to raise, I suggest that you have "tough love" tattooed someplace real prominent on your body so that you won't forget it. Like across your forehead. I think branding would actually be better, because you could feel it as well as see it.

Tough love means that you will do whatever it takes to make your child a success. The secret is the word tough. It really applies to YOU, not your child. You better be tough. If crying, begging or whining pushes your buttons, don't become a parent. Or school teacher for that matter. Because you will cave in like a cardboard house in a thunderstorm. When you cave in, you are training that child to be a whining, complaining, dysfunctional, miserable adult. And boy, aren't they fun to be around? You'll see as you get older. They're called co-workers.

I have a concrete suggestion. Once a decision is made, stick with it and don't let the child whine or beg. Cut the conversation off immediately, to return when a normal tone of voice returns. This is one of those "don't do this" real life stories. "Mom, may I have an ice cream bar?" "No, honey, it's too close to dinner." "But, Mom, I'm hungry and dinner is almost an hour away." "No, ice cream is not to be eaten until after dinner." "I'll eat all my dinner, I promise." "Listen, honey, I've got work to do. Please go and watch television." "But I'm hungry, Mom. Please let me have an ice cream bar. I'll be quiet and I promise I'll eat my dinner." "Oh, O.K., go ahead. But don't disturb me until dinner." "Yes, Mom," as she skips merrily off to get her hard-earned ice cream bar. What you just witnessed was the building of a Frankenstein Monster, without all the messy body parts. Like it or not, every adult, and especially every parent is a ROLE MODEL. The monkey see, monkey do principal in living color, everyday. What did this well meaning and hard working mother just teach her child? . . . . You got it. That she doesn't mean what she says. That her mind can be changed, which guarantees what kind of response from the child? . . . . That's right. An argument. Every time. How's that child going to respond in school when the teacher asks her to do something? "Connie, your assignment tonight is page 56, #1-30. What's that? No, #1-15 will not suffice.

Yes, I'm sure that #1-15 is probably enough to show competency but I asked for #1-30 for a reason. There are other competencies in the latter 15 that I want to check. No, doing #10-20 is not an option either." And so it goes.

There was an experiment done with chickens that illustrates this point so clearly that I still marvel at it. The scientists wanted to see what the optimum reward system is to keep a chicken begging for food the longest. All the chickens had a button to peck to receive a food pellet. One set of chickens got rewarded with every peck, one set every two pecks, one set every three pecks, etc., all the way to one pellet for every ten pecks. They were trained for a long time to respond to this exact reward system. Then the scientist stopped giving any food pellets. Now the experiment starts. Which chicken do you think pecked the longest in its now futile search for food? Think about it for a minute . . . . Yes? . . . . How about you young man? . . . . Interesting. Young lady? . . . . Very interesting . You're on the right track. What we actually had was this: The chicken that was used to a consistent reward system, one peck, one pellet, quit wasting his time first. He knew that nothing was coming, so he quit trying. The one with the next most consistent reward system, two pecks for one pellet, soon after stopped trying. The lesson to be learned, as parents, is that the chicken who got rewarded very inconsistently, the ratio being seven pecks for every one pellet, kept pecking the button almost forever after the food stopped. Is probably still pecking now, as we speak. "Mommy, can I have some ice cream?" "No. No. No. No. No. No. Oh, all right, just make sure it doesn't spoil your dinner." BINGO. That child has just sprouted feathers. She is chicken number seven. She will never accept what she is told without an argument. She is probably still arguing about the pay raise that she didn't get ten years ago. So, to save your child's adulthood, wear that tough love brand on your forehead proudly and mean it. Always be consistent with your children.

To help with the consistency deal, there are a few rules that you and your spouse need to discuss and agree on before you ever ask your child to do one, single, thing.

Don't ever say or promise the child anything before OK'ing it with your spouse first. Have these discussions away from the child.

If you say something like, "You know, it seems like a good day to go to the movies," and the child can hear you, you are in fact going to the movies that day, good day or not. Don't make suggestions of any kind within earshot of a child, because then they are no longer suggestions. In that child's mind they are a reality. You have now put yourself in a terrible position. You either end up doing something that, in retrospect, wasn't a great idea, like losing your job because you told junior that you would take him to a ball game during the day. Or you have to change your mind, in which case you have set yourself up for a wrestling match with your child, which could easily morph into the tag-team match from Hades if your darling spouse is also angry at whatever stupid thing came out of your mouth. Adults are so used to speaking to other adults and weighing whether that person is a liar or just a politician that we have a tendency to forget that most children, for a period of time, actually believe that what an adult says is the truth. I'm still stewing over the fact that, when I was ten years old, I was promised one dollar per plug of Zoisia Grass that I helped my father and a neighbor put in. It never occurred to me that the neighbor was "just joking," as my father put it the next day. I thought that maybe I was born defective, not having a sense of humor and all, because I didn't see what was funny about getting gypped out of two hundred dollars. As a matter of fact, I still don't. I STILL want my money, and my trust in adults, back. Right now I'd settle for the money.

On a similar note, it is always best to think before you speak, especially if you are going to make a request or demand of your child. DON'T say things you don't mean, because you have got to go through with what has just escaped from your mouth; otherwise you have just gone from consistent parent to poultry farmer, wondering why your chickens won't listen to you. "Go to your room and finish all of your homework. I don't care that it's five hours worth. You are not having dinner until you have finished. And if it's not done by morning, no breakfast, either." Now, Mr. Big Man, you have just stuffed yourself into a box in which you can't possibly fit. You have made two huge mistakes. You have said words that you will have to eat later, which may be just as well, because it's probably the only dinner that you are going to get anyway. The other mistake is not noticing that your wife is behind you cutting vegetables with a sharp knife while you are making a fool out of yourself screaming at her only child.

There is actually a third mistake here and that is punishing in anger. Anger is the beast that drives bad parenting and bad teaching. Everybody gets angry but nobody thinks clearly when upset. The best antidote for parenting by anger is to have a plan for what to do when a child needs correction. The plan is best developed before he needs correction. You know that your child is going to mess up, so don't be shocked by it. Just be ready for it, that's all. I read a quote by Plato or Socrates years ago, which for me puts everything in perspective. I guess that some ancient teenage hoodlum had done something to infuriate the great one, because he went on a rant about how disrespectful, violent, disobedient, lazy and generally worthless teenagers were. He went on to mention that they were not only a threat to society, but threatened the very existence of civilization itself. I thought to myself, how refreshing. It says to me that children have always been children and will always be children, for good or for bad. So if you are shocked by misbehaviors, don't be a parent, teacher, or any other profession dealing with children because misbehaving is what psychiatrists call normal. It is your response to it that separates good parent from bad, good teacher from bad, good police officer from bad.

Sit down with your spouse and concoct a misbehavior correction plan. Don't wait until you get a call from the police department to come pick your son up to formulate your plan. That plan will probably have elements in it that are frowned upon by most judicial systems, such as pain and death. So come up with a plan. When Cheryl acts out in public, what will we do? Spanking is a very limited option, should be used only for open defiance, should be given as a choice that the child is going to make, and used very infrequently. In public it is not an option at all, unless you enjoy explaining to a SWAT team why you are having to discipline your child. A good option is removal. Instant and swift. The secret to any effective discipline is instant and swift. That's the power of a proper spanking, as opposed to a beating. It is not the pain that is the prime motivating tool. So, if your child throws a fit in a store over something that he feels that he is entitled to and you are refusing to buy because, unlike the adults he sees on TV, you are not a millionaire, simply declare the shopping excursion over and march him promptly out of the store, kicking and screaming. I prefer throwing him over my shoulder for dramatic effect, but that is just a style preference. Either way, the child is stunned by the forcefulness of your actions and usually taken aback by the rounds of applause that will spontaneously burst forth from other adults in the store, who are also sick of hearing him whine and relieved that at least SOMEBODY out there is taking the time to raise his child properly. Explain to the child that the ticket to public places is proper behavior, and he will have the PRIVILEGE of going to public places when, and only when, he can act accordingly. The learning curve is even more electric if you pick your places of removal cunningly. Removal from a birthday party at Chuck E. Cheese is a mind blower. The child will learn more in five minutes than thirty hours of father-son lectures. The trick is to PLAN to do this, or anything similar. If your child has been misbehaving lately, take him to someplace that he would like to go, but one in which you have no real interest in. When he is removed, it has cost you nothing and him everything.

Removal of PRIVILEGES is another good tool. What is a privilege? Anything except food, water, air and shelter. Take the TV, toys, electronic equipment of any kind. Whatever. I have a form at school that I hand to parents of teenagers. All a parent has to do is sign it and the form goes straight to the highway patrol department. The child will NEVER get a driver's license until the parent signs a release form. Now, THAT is an attention getter . . . . Proper etiquette states that it is never polite to boo the professor. Evidently we are forgetting why it is that we are disciplining a child. Parenting is WORK, with a capitol "W," and all of this work is to ensure that a child becomes a successful adult, whether they particularly like it or not. The hardest part about parenting, especially for very young parents, is that everything you do needs to fit into a long term, goal oriented plan. If you are almost a child your own self, that is a very hard mental leap to make, because the younger you are, the more short term goal oriented you are. A perfect example is a budget. Young lady, what does your budget look like? . . . . Of course you don't have one. You should have one, but you don't. You're only fourteen. I am fifty four. I have one. You're thinking changes as you get older.

Back to practical success oriented discipline tips. It is very important that the adults in the family communicate with each other and stay on the same page. That includes grandma. Children will look for the weakest link in the fence to try to escape parental authority. Don't let a child play one adult against the other. They will play them better than they do their Gameboy. If your child comes running to you from the direction of another adult asking for something, what you don't say is "yes." They are running from that adult because they just said "no" and are coming to you because you look like a sucker. What you ask is, "What did mommy say?" And stick with it. The parents may want to have a private discussion later about what mommy said, but mom and dad and uncle and grandma need to back each other up in front of that child. Consistency. Clear vision. Clear expectations. Family unity. Family purpose.

We are at an interesting point in history. A well functioning family is needed more than ever now, and yet they seem to be harder and harder to find. There are a couple of things going on in the background that are contributing to this. One is a divorce rate so high that most kids have never seen how a family is supposed to work. In the famous marital advice given to a newlywed by Ed Norton from the Honeymooners, "If you don't want to fight, what are you getting married for?" Another trend is economic. This idea of the "working poor" is ridiculous. Pay scales so low that people have to work five jobs to stay afloat, while nobody is left at home to give any kind of guidance to their children. A long time ago it was called slavery but that term has a slightly negative connotation these days, so corporations call it "working poor" instead. It used to be that if you had a latchkey kid you would be put in the system for child abandonment. Now it's O.K. to leave your children alone, raised by violent and disrespectful and destructive images coming off of the surrogate parent, the TV screen, because profits have become more important than our own children. So, do what you can to create your own, real, loving family unit, because that is the best defense you and your child will have against an increasingly cold world.

"Whew. Let the professor sit for a second after that rant. Boy, I feel better now. Sometimes it feels good to get stuff off your chest. Whew, again. Why don't we take a ten minute bathroom break and then we'll wrap this up so that you can spend the rest of your Saturday in deep meditative contemplation. Or wild abandonment. Whatever . . . .

Alright, let's wrap this bad boy up. I appreciate your attentiveness today. It is my hope that somewhere in the midst of all this boring mishmash that you have learned something of value today that you can carry home with you. Now that you have raised your child well and prepared him as best you can to be a success in school, what do you do once he is actually in school? My best advice is two-fold. First, I would get to know the teachers personally, as human beings. Invite them over for dinner. Teachers are poor. They love free dinners. Once a bond is established, then you've got a group of human beings doing their best for your child, which is all that one can ask. It also rephrases the "What are you doing to my child?" to "What did my child do to you and how far should I throw him?," which is music to a teacher's ears. Now you've got a REAL bond established. Which brings me to my second word of advice. Let them do their job.

I have a friend named Nicole, who got a call from her son's school one morning, asking her to come to the school because her son was disrupting class. She was furious, at both the school and teacher, for making her get off work. The fact that she herself was a teacher meant that she, of all people, should know better, but teacher does not trump being a human being and a mother, so off she went: good teacher to do battle with bad, incompetent, unfit to be a janitor teacher. She is escorted to the child's room and peers into the little classroom window before storming in to tell the incompetent off, when she spots her son. I quote here. "He was standing on top of the desk, acting like a stone fool." Welcome to the wonderful world of the teacher. Nicole said that she became a good parent that day. Let the teachers do their jobs. DO NOT PROTECT YOUR CHILD FROM THE CONSEQUENCES OF THEIR OWN MISBEHAVIOR or else they will never learn anything. You will be backing down the teacher, then backing down the administrators, then backing down the police officer, then backing down the probation officer and then you are going to be trying to back down the state prosecutor, who apparently doesn't know what back down means. He is a dolt. And you have lost your child forever. This can all be avoided. Do not shield your child from deserved punishment.

The last thing you do as a good parent is to hand your parent role to other good adults that are in your child's life and let them do their best. Have faith. My son called me from school one time, explaining that he had after school detention. I said "Oh?" and picked him up after school. I asked him why I was being asked to spend my valuable time being chauffeur and his explanation went like this: "Dad, the teacher is such a jerk. Nobody likes him." I said, "What did the jerk ask you to do?" "He asked me to stop talking during class. But . . . ." "Did you, in fact, stop talking in class?" My son is a very bright child, bright enough to be a lawyer. He could sense that his case was going south at light speed. "No. But everybody else was talking and nobody was paying attention to the man any and . . . ." At this time his voice was trailing off into nothingness. If you are a good teacher you don't need words to convey complex meaning. The proper stare with the proper attitude will suffice nicely. I am a particularly good teacher. Once he was silent I decided to speak. "Son, you know I love you. You are going to be a great chef when you get older, just as you say you are. I have one word of advice. If a teacher-even the most incompetent, lame, drooling, foolish, ignorant, boring and detestable joke of a teacher on the planet-one who in fact forged his teacher certificate—asks you to do anything, up to and including setting your hair on fire, you are going to do it. DO YOU UNDERSTAND ME? As I have said before, children are sensitive and have an uncanny ability to pick up the most subtle of messages. All I know is that I never got a call from the school again.

The thing about being overprotective is the silent message that you are sending to your child. It is that, in reality, you don't have faith that she can do anything on her own. If you keep hovering over her, you're probably right. Instead of being a launching pad to greatness, you will become a crutch, something to lean on while complaining about the day's failures. I still remember the day I got my first flat tire. I was in my teens and was out on a date. I was acting the big man until I heard the flopping of the tire and pulled over. My first instinct was to call Dad. I had gone from big man to medium sized boy in the blink of an eye. My father did me a huge favor that day. He told me where the jack was, then hung up. After a half an hour I was the big man again, to stay. False praise and overprotection does not instill a sense of man or womanhood. Concrete, actual successful accomplishments do. The more successful accomplishments that you can provide for your child as they are growing up, the more of a man or woman you will have later on in life. So, now you have got the home thing and school thing going on. What can possibly derail your child from being a successful adult? He is bright, happy, intelligent, caring, self-motivated, so handsome that Denzel Washington or Richard Gere are jealous. What could possibly go wrong? The entire media empire set up to make money off of destroying your child is one thing. Another is their "friends" who have watched one video too many, drenched in sex, violence, disrespect, criminality and rampant materialism, until they think that this pirate fantasy world is real. And now they are your child's best friend. The parent's question is, who is going to influence whom?

This friend business is very important to study closely, because, after a certain age, the "friend" has a lot more influence on your child than you do. So, even though the child will scream with indignation that it is none of your business, press on with getting to know who these friends are, because it is in fact your most important business of the day. So, who does your child hang out with? You can tell a lot by checking out their aforementioned tattoos. Does the tattoo have meaning? Does it look like a doctor bending over a microscope doing cancer research, or does it lean more towards a dagger inserted through a skull? Is it a cute butterfly placed strategically on the lower back or is it a mural of snakes eating infants displayed across the chest and down both arms? These give a clue as to a person's outlook on life. Devils anywhere on the body, no matter how minute, are a bad sign. Hair styles are another clue, but murkier to read. Every generation goes through phases guaranteed to drive the previous generation crazy. I can live with the hair thing. I remember when my uncle came home with a Mohawk haircut once. My grandfather, who was a career military man, was not amused. Upon threats of death my uncle changed his hairstyle. He came back with a Cossack, which is a shrunk up version of the Mohawk, and looks even worse. A lot of the black kids at school used to cut their initials in their hair. I have a high tolerance for strange hair, as long as it doesn't show disrespect. If the letters in their head didn't spell a word that is banned off the public airwaves, I could live with it if their parents could. One time my son came with his mother, sporting a brand new haircut called the rat tail. How fitting.

Drug abuse is a whole different ball game. Watch how your child acts while waiting for their "friend" to arrive. If they are calmly doing their homework, that is one thing. If they are continuously rocking back and forth like the pitching coach Leo Mazzoni in the ninth inning, that is not good. If they are chewing on their hand and making growling sounds, you better hope their friend gets there quick.

Know who your child's friends are. And know where they are. Don't win the trifecta like a frantic parent who returned a call to me at the school. Her son had been skipping and I wanted to know what was up. She said that she hadn't seen her son in two weeks. He was living somewhere, and I am not making this up, "down the street with a kid that she couldn't remember the name of, except that his nickname was "Spider."

What happens when there is no real functioning family unit at the house? The child will create his own family unit, except without the word functioning anywhere to be seen. This family is called a gang. The desire to belong is almost as strong as the desire to eat, and a child will belong to something, somewhere. The children who are so alienated that they actually feel that they don't belong ANYWHERE are the ones who shoot the school up. I suggest that you do everything in your power to make that child feel like a productive member of a FAMILY. If they are a member of a family, then you have certain rights as a parent, like the right to ask "Where are you going, who with, what are you planning on doing and when are you getting home?" The decibel level of their shrieking will inform you of how tight of a leash you need to keep on them so that they will survive long enough to become that successful adult that you keep harping about.

I was reading an article about the movie star Al Pacino. It stated that he grew up in a tough neighborhood and was often angry at his mother because, in his mind, she was the worst mother on the planet. Instead of letting little Al go outside and play with his hoodlum friends she insisted on him staying inside and completing his schoolwork. This set Al up for years of ridicule. He was a sissy boy and his mother was a domineering, pig headed old witch. Al the movie star will tell you this: Many of those friends who kept yelling for him to come out and play are either dead or in jail. Al Pacino the movie star would not exist today if it wasn't for a mother who was stronger and more focused than most. Mr. Pacino knows this. He said that she saved his life. It is how you raise your child when they are very young, and the parent-child RELATIONSHIP and bond that you develop early that will allow both parent and child to survive the teenage years.

There you have it. It's two o'clock. Time sure does fly when you're having fun. Before you go, I want to say a couple of things to you personally. You are all good kids. I can tell by the look in your eyes. Don't have children before you are ready. I'm not worried about the fate of the babies right now. I am worried about your fate. There is so much potential for greatness in this room. Some of you will end up saving lives in your various professions. Your greatness knows no boundaries. You can destroy all that in one single unguarded moment. If you have a child too early, YOUR LIFE AS YOU KNOW IT IS OVER. Altered forever. And you will spend the rest of it trying to dig yourself and your child out of a poverty hole. That is going to be a tough climb. Respect yourself. Have faith in yourself. You deserve better than that. The world deserves better than that. It needs your greatness today, more so than ever before. Be there to meet your destiny. Don't take yourself out of the picture. Be there when it is your time. And parent smartly so that your child will be there when it is their time. May God bless you and help you make good choices. Enjoy the rest of your weekend. It has been my pleasure to have been here today.

Introduction to "Rethinking Education: Newspaper Columns on Parenting"

I wrote my first "Rethinking Education" newspaper column on March 19, 2015. It was entitled "The Stress-Free Diploma" and was about the unhealthy amount of stress put upon students today, which is often counter-productive to what I would consider a real education. Three and a half years and 160 columns later I am still discussing what I consider to be the important issues of the day as far as educating children are concerned. I have 40 years of experience in teaching children, many coming from disadvantaged backgrounds, and believe in using my experience to make schools a better place for children. I believe that all children can succeed, no matter what their circumstances, and try to shed light on how teachers and schools can better make this happen.

Since parents are, in fact, the child's first teacher, I sometimes gear my column directly to parents and give advice on what they can do in the household to further the academic and emotional success of their children. Early, and I mean real early, childhood experiences have a huge impact on children later on in life and if parents are given the tools to shape those early experiences in a positive and beneficial way, they will have the building blocks to create a successful child who will stand a real good chance of becoming a successful adult. This is every parents dream and hope.

The beauty is that none of this costs money. It just takes understanding. Any parent, anywhere, at anytime, can be a successful parent. I have included in this book a few articles that are directed to parents that might give them insight into creating a successful child. That is my dream and my hope.

A Roadmap to Peace: Toddlers, Rage and Words
Gadsden County Times – 2/5/18

I still laugh when I pull out an old picture of my sister and her cousin when they were both between the ages of two and three. There they were, sitting in a bath tub together. They both had a handful of each other's hair and were apparently screaming at the top of each other's lungs. So much for conflict resolution in the world of the toddler. Conflict resolution and the possibility of living in a peaceful world is one of the greatest challenges of the human race. Adults can learn a lot about the subject by spending some time studying the behavior of three-year olds. The age of three is where it is all happening. The child has left toddlerhood and now has increasingly coordinated physical skills and a brain that is working overtime at absorbing new information. Vocabulary and speech ability are exploding and those that hardly talked before are blathering away like a magpie working on its eighth cup of coffee. One of the main areas of growth for a three-year old is in socialization – getting along with others. This getting along thing is taking on increasing importance in modern society because more and more children are not at home anymore at the age of three, but are put in mass settings – pre-k environments – because both parents (if there are two) feel the necessity to work. (The ramifications of millions of parents working for low wages are many, but children being raised in mass settings out of necessity is an important one.) Safety is job one for any pre-k teacher, and how safe the classroom environment depends a lot on the socialization level of each child. Tell four three - year olds to simply just "go play together" and see what happens. After about three minutes it may not resemble "play" at all. Assault and battery, maybe.

The act of "playing together," much less "playing nice together" is stunningly complicated. Add in the foreign concept of "sharing" and what you've got is a big dose of "Are you kidding me?" in the child's head. Three-year olds are transitioning from a world where they are the center of the universe (Mine, mine mine – which applies to everything, mine or not) to the shocking realization that they are not. And then they are supposed to get along with all of these other children who are also coming to the same appalling, unsettling realization. The other key thing to note is that they are transitioning from a pre-verbal world of brute force to get your way to one in which you are supposed to ask for what you want. This is a huge and important difference. As a matter of fact, the use of words makes all of the difference in the world. Since a pre-verbal child can't articulate anything, their recourse comes from this menu: snatching, hitting, crying, screaming, or the sophisticated pointing and screaming. Actually, if a child is pointing and screaming before they run over and hit somebody, that is communication that you can build on. And you build on it through methodical speech development. Another key point is that not all three-year olds are the same. The maturation difference between children at that age can be enormous. Some can say, "Mr. Bill, Sarah is encroaching on my playhouse area and I wish that she could move over slightly so that we can both have fun. I would prefer that my blocks didn't get knocked over." With others, the conversation is more like "shriek – wham! – crying." To produce peaceful conflict resolution, children must be carefully and consistently guided to use words to not just articulate their feelings, but actually see positive results from it. When a teacher hears the first rumblings of disaster, they will immediately go to the conflict area and ask something like "What do you want, I'll help you?" and guide the child through their ramblings, rantings or screechings to a point of understanding, and then, upon understanding, resolve the conflict. As children are able to get their problems solved through verbal articulation instead of violence, and then rewarded for it, the violence and conflict will slowly disappear. Older children and adults: Take a hint.

All Children Are Scientists
Tallahassee Democrat – 7/13/16
Gadsden County Times – 7/14/16

If it weren't so sad, I'd laugh out loud every time I hear that schools need to find a way to get more children, especially girls, interested in the sciences. Are you kidding me? All children are scientists. What schools need to do to get children interested in the sciences as they get older is not bore them, or punish them with bad grades, or otherwise, somehow, ruin the science experience for them. Quite simply, schools have all the budding scientists that they need. The elementary schools are chock full of them. Stop turning children off to science. It is impossible for the often heard statement "I hate science" to be true, because the study of science is the study of every single fascinating thing on this planet, or solar system or universe, or possible multiple universes. What the child really means is "I hate what went on in my science class." Now, that can be true.

Parents, you have the opportunity every day, but especially on weekends, holidays, or summers, to build your scientist at home, one who has the possibility of learning enough science to help make the world a better place and earn a really good income at the same time. I am serious. Sports are great, but are seen by many children as the only avenue to making real money. My advice is to not only run outside to play catch, but carry a couple of magnifying glasses with you for some serious fun afterwards. Parents, you will find that your average three year old, if given the chance to explore things with a magnifying glass, binoculars or telescope, will choose them over playing with a ball 7 out of ten times. This is because these tools have something to offer any child, any real scientist, that the ball can't and those are moments of jaw-dropping wonder.

A three year old is a natural scientist because every waking moment is filled with new discoveries about the world, the excitement of discovery and the quest for more. They ask four questions all the time: Why, why, why, and occasionally, why? (They will also fight a nap tooth and nail because, heaven forbid, they might miss something.) Adults have been jaded by real life so much that they don't have many "I can't believe this" wonder moments in their life anymore, which is at the heart of being a child and a scientist. Providing those wonder moments and then explaining is all you need to create scientists for life.

A case in point was this Fourth of July. I happened to be sitting on the banks of the Apalachicola River in Chattahoochee watching the fireworks go off. A three year old was near me and literally was out of his mind with joy. He was shrieking that he loved fireworks and I fully believed him. This is what an educator would call "a teachable moment." Why did you hear an echo coming from off of the bridge? (Sound waves.) Why did I see the flash before I heard the boom? (Speed of light.) "What made the rocket shoot up like that?" (Propulsion.) Speaking of propulsion, I taught at a Head Start program for three year olds and taught them "propulsion" in 15 seconds. I blew up a balloon and let it go flying around the room and as they were squealing in delight had them chant "Propulsion, propulsion." Build a sand castle and have them chant "erosion, erosion" at the top of their lungs as they destroy it with a water hose. They love it, which is the whole point. If a child loves doing something their brain absorbs information at a stunning rate. If a child is thrilled by discovery, they will learn in one minute what they may possibly get out of a textbook in an hour. I remember looking through a microscope at prepared slides of human blood cells, muscle cells and plant cells and was just blown away at both their similarities and differences. As an adult I had a wonder moment when I looked through a telescope in my backyard that a friend had brought over and I marveled at the sight of the rings around Saturn. I could not believe what I was seeing.

So, parents, strike while the iron is hot and the child is young. Turn off the TV, grab that magnifying glass and run outside and stare at bugs, or leaves, or flowers. Point the binoculars at that crazy looking bird. Examine water under a microscope. Point the telescope at the stars. And somebody write a memo to the one percent that there should be public lending "libraries" where ordinary people can check out this equipment on a weekly basis, just like a book. In the meantime, do the best that you can. When your child grows up to invent or discover something important, she will hug you for your efforts when she was small.

DETAILS AND BRAIN DEVELOPMENT
GADSDEN COUNTY TIMES – 5/10/18

One of the best things for brain development in young children, whether at home or at school, is to get them to focus on small details. Children have a built-in radar for small details, but often it is of the irrelevant sort, such as when you spend ten minutes in a serious conversation with a child and at the end you realize that they haven't heard a word that you said because they have been focusing on the minute speck of lint on your shirt. What I am talking about is training the brain to purposely look for and notice small details, which will pay huge dividends in school later on in many different ways.

As always, the best path for learning in young children can come in the form of games and fun. One way to train for details is the old set up where you have two almost identical pictures side by side, but the second picture has been changed in several slight ways. The child has to scour the picture and circle what is different. They love this. A variation on this is to take a child, or a doll, and have the children stare at their clothing, then everyone close their eyes (good luck with that) and when they reopen them they have to figure out which piece of clothing has changed. Or have a child go into a certain portion of the room and remove something (or add something) and everyone has to guess what it was.

Puzzles are still my go-to favorite for children attending to details. They can look for pieces that match by color, or subject ("Yes, that looks like it is part of the tree") or shape. The beauty is that the brain has to attend to several details at once to make it work. A child may find a piece that matches the color and subject matter, but still has to deal the shape to make the piece fit right. This multi-dimensional attention to detail plays out every time a child gets two pieces that they know go together, but then has to keep moving the pieces around and around until they are in place. Puzzles carry the added weight of having the child physically manipulate the details in front of them, as opposed to just looking. It also builds patience because smashing the square peg into the round hole doesn't ever seem to work.

Loaded wise-guy type of questions work wonders on a child's ability to articulate detail. Adult: (looking at a picture of a duck) "I think that it is an eagle." Child: (Incredulous) "What? That's a duck." Adult: No it's not, it's an eagle." Child: (Voice rising in pitch, tone and volume) "It's a duck!!!" Adult: "I think you have gone crazy. What in the world makes you think that this is a duck and not an eagle?" (Now the adult has the child exactly where he wants him – in full tilt lawyer mode.) "That's a duck – see the webbed feet. Eagles don't have webbed feet, they have talons. Look at that – the duck has a bill. The eagle doesn't have a bill, it has a beak, and a sharp one at that. And look at those feathers…." And the details in comparison just keep on rolling out. Bingo. Now, most small children aren't precocious enough to use the word "talon" but you will catch their drift when they point out that only an idiot would think that an eagle has webbed feet.

What every teacher on this planet loves is when a child kicks into lawyer mode – backing a point of view with a myriad of relevant details. Now we are talking higher level thinking that will pay off in any profession. Attention to detail can be taught in a hundred creative ways. "Let's go outside and look for a four leaf clover." Or, when a child only has the word "blue" in her vocabulary, post a chart with twenty different shades of blue. Soon you will get "I believe that blue is too dark – I think I will go with azure for the sky" as she is coloring away and the adult is racing to the bookshelf for the dictionary. It's all in the details.

Discussing Homework
Tallahassee Democrat – 9/16/15
Gadsden County Times – 9/24/15

Homework. As a topic, it seems innocent enough. Almost all school children, parents and teachers have to deal with it in some form or another. I have taught school for decades and the longer I have taught and the more interactions that I have had with children and parents, the more I have come to realize that the topic of homework is probably one of the most controversial ones in education. It is so controversial that nobody ever really talks about it in a systematic way, it is just simply done haphazardly, according to desires of the individual educator. This is a shame, because homework can have serious implications for all involved, sometimes positive, sometimes negative. I, personally am very conflicted on the topic, so I am not sure that I have any answers. I do have a series of questions, however, that should shed light on the subject. Here we go.

How much is too much? Since homework is not necessarily coordinated in a school, teacher "A" may give 30 minutes worth in math, then teacher "B" gives twenty and before you know it, the child had three hours of homework after he has already put in a full day at the factory. Is this right? Some parents are bewildered because their child never has homework and they are trying to structure their evening so that there is more than just watching television.

What if a child can't do the homework? She doesn't understand it? What if the parent can't really help? I have seen terrible fights, verbal and physical, go on in households over homework. Some households are under tremendous amounts of negative stress, either economically or emotionally and the added stress of missed assignments or poorly done work thrust upon a frustrated parent or child can be the tipping point for some very unpleasant experiences. Learning should not be unpleasant, whether at school or at home.

What if there is literally nobody there to help a child with their homework? If a child can already do the work, what is the point of giving it? And if a child needs a little help with it, what happens if there is nobody there to ask for it or to check it? It is not a child's fault that, for whatever reason, there are very few adults around with time for them. Some parents work multiple jobs, many are single parents, many have multiple children. What you don't want is a child doing poor work at home, and bad habits develop that have to be undone back in the classroom. If work is done in the classroom, it is supervised and guided by a teacher. At the house, you have no idea of the level of supervision and guidance.

What right does a school have to reach into a household AFTER school hours and dictate what goes on in that home? What if a parent doesn't get to see their child very much and wants to simply play with that child during their time together? Or travel? Or whatever? I have seen it where sometimes when too much homework is given, it warps the family into constantly worrying about school work instead of just being a family. A parent needs to be able to dictate the quality of their home life.

What right does the school have to dictate to teachers about their life AFTER school hours? Why should some teachers take home a boatload of work to be done after school? The school day is tiring enough as it is.

Speaking of tiring, children are children. Every child has only so much learning capacity for a day, or an hour. Trying to jam more into a child after they have reached their capacity is often counterproductive, and leads to burn out. You don't want a child's school experience to be that of a gerbil on a treadmill. Teachers neither.

It is interesting that in many parts of Europe where children perform high academically there is a large anti-homework movement. In parts of Asia, conversely, they work their children relentlessly, who also perform high in academics. The stress levels among their children is sometimes very high and has negative consequences. I believe the answer is somewhere in the middle.

So, what to do? I have taught for decades in economically depressed areas and have had the privilege to serve hundreds of parents who are wonderful people. I know the stressors that are in the households that are struggling. I did not want to add to that stress, but be a help for the family. These are my homework suggestions:

As a teacher, I always taught as if the child had no parents. I assumed that they were going to get most of their education in the class and demanded their best while they were sitting in my classroom. If I got a good hour or day from my students, very seldom did I send anything home that was mandatory in the form of homework. I got their best and they had done a good job that day. I didn't want to deal with the negative consequences of poorly done and unguided work at the house.

Notice I said "mandatory." This is the key to opening the door for those parents that have the time and want a certain amount of academics to take place in the home after school, while at the same time not putting unneeded added pressure on households that can't take any more. Instead of homework, call it extra-credit and it is voluntary, allowing each parent to control their home life. (It is all positive, taking the negative consequences of failure off of the table.) Each child can have a reading assignment so that if a parent wants to structure reading time into their evening, they can do so. Each child can have short worksheets on the work that they have been doing recently and can complete them to show mastery. Parents can ask questions on the sheet if there is misunderstanding, which will be clarified the next day in class. There are all kinds of creative ways that you can structure "homework" so that you get the best that each family has to offer in a positive way, which is to simply give the parent the ability to control their time at home with their children without punishment. Most parents and children will do their best for what they are able to do and the teacher is always there to provide their best, which is doubly important for those children who need more adult supervision. When schools and families support each other they get the best out of their children, which is what it is all about.

Emphasize Critical Thinking
Tallahassee Democrat – 11/8/17

It is time for schools to shine a spotlight on critical thinking skills – a large, stadium bright type of spotlight. Webster defines critical thinking as "exercising or involving careful judgment or judicious evaluation – thinking." As the modern world gets increasingly more complex and in a sense more ominous it is imperative for the well-being of our society that its members are able to think clearly and critically when it comes to creating, inventing and problem solving. Schools need to provide critical thinking skill training from pre-k on up, so that upon graduation each child has the ability to face the challenges of the day. These skills can be applied to all subject matter in school and brought to bear upon dealing constructively with life's difficulties in adulthood.

There are several components to critical thinking. One of them is the ability to separate fact from fiction. What is a fact? Again, going to Webster, it is "actuality – hinges on evidence." The scientific method is based on theories becoming "facts" by presenting verifiable, duplicable evidence of existence. Over time these "facts" are tested and retested, sometimes changing as new evidence is produced. Children need to ask questions like "Where did this fact come from? Is it verifiable? Is this source legitimate? How many sources agree with this? Can I cross-reference this? What can be said about the disagreements that may arise? Why aren't they right?" At the end of the day, when looked at critically, a student can have some solid "facts" on which to base opinions and actions.

Speaking of opinions, the second component is to be able to separate them from facts. Hopefully, one's opinions are based on facts, but that is obviously not necessarily so and children need to learn the difference between the two. Opinions are perfectly fine, are in fact what makes each one of us unique, but are often a blend of our own view of facts mixed in with our emotional responses to them. To take it even further, emotional responses are exactly what a lot of opinions are aimed at, and if a person is responding emotionally to something, the opinion maker has just bypassed the need for "facts."

Beyond facts and opinions is propaganda. Children need to learn how to recognize it as a whole separate realm of "information." It goes beyond analyzing what is being said into the realm of why it is being said. It is important to be understood that there are many people out there who aren't as concerned about facts as they are about shaping your opinion about something. Shaping another's opinion goes way beyond just shoddy salesmen, but into the realm of economics, politics, science, religion – you name it - and behind it all is the fight over really big money and power.

People are bombarded daily by a myriad of media outlets as well as print. This is getting to be overwhelming, and in a very real way, dangerous. In pre-electronic times, information was more easily verifiable when it was just print media. It was static and permanent and much easier to mull over, debate and come to a conclusion. With the advent of electronic media, everything changed. Whole media empires are built on shaping opinions through mass media, because audio and visual images are a lot harder to critically analyze, especially if they are pouring out in a continuous stream.

Children need to be taught how to verify facts, how to go to different sources for information, and how to analyze the legitimacy of those sources. They have got to be given the tools to think for themselves and form their own opinions based on facts. An intelligent and informed citizenry is the rock-bed of any democracy, and is exactly what Thomas Jefferson had in mind when promoting public schools.

Gifts, Children and Education
Gadsden County Times – 12/14/17

Gift giving is an integral part of many religious holidays, often especially focusing on children. The joy of giving a child something that makes them happy is one of life's great pleasures. So, as parents are pondering what to give children, what are the thoughts that run through their head when they hear, "I think that I am going to get my child something educational. I think that she would like that."

Some parents would step slowly back from the crazy person. Others may laugh out loud. Others may take pity on the misguided parent with some sage advice such as, "Oh, your child doesn't want to get anything that reminds them of school. Give them something fun."

This attitude, whether overt or subtle, speaks volumes about our society's view of education, school and children. There is a lot to deconstruct here, so we'll start with school itself.

School is viewed by many as a place for work, not fun. And by work, we don't mean work in the good sense of purposeful, pleasurable and meaningful. More like the minimum wage view of work: dull, monotonous, meaningless, joyless, and boring. To others it is hard, painful and confusing. School is someplace that a child would rather not be. Anywhere but there. Any toy but an educational toy.

A jaundiced view of school gives us a jaundiced view of the educational process and warps our view of what learning really is. Here is a flash bulletin: learning and school are not necessarily the same things. School carries so much excess baggage that even Albert Einstein remarked that he had to take a year off after his schooling just to wash the distaste of it out of his mouth. (I'm paraphrasing, but it's true.)

So, what is learning to a child? It is the pure essence and very definition of childhood. It is the discovery of new things. The discovery and understanding of new things is the most joyful thing that a brain can engage in. Real learning turns the brain into not only an efficient reasoning, computing machine but also a fountain of happiness. "Look at that! It's a fox! Did you see the fox?!" "What are those squiggly little things I see under this microscope? They're what!? You're kidding?" "What do you mean bats saved Great Britain during WWII? What does that have to do with radar?" "Wow. There's a ring around the moon! Why is that?" Or when a child reads their first actual sentence and then goes berserk running around the room, drunk with their new-found power and ability. Or when a child sees snow for the first time. Or the beach for the first time. Or looks through the Hubble telescope. Memo to adults: if you want to experience exactly the excitement that a child feels upon discovery and learning look at pictures from the Hubble telescope. It will blow your mind and keep blowing it the more you think about what you are seeing. And it will imbed deeply inside of you what real learning should be about. That's the feeling you are shooting for inside a child's mind. It should the feeling that you are shooting for inside of a schoolhouse. In short, learning new things is exactly what your brain considers "fun."

The green light is now on for parents to give "educational" gifts to children, because in reality education and fun are the same thing. Children may or may not enjoy their school experience, but all children love learning. So give them some fun: Books, robotic sets, art supplies, electronic kits, chemistry sets, musical instruments, puzzles, Legos and Lincoln logs, magnifying glasses and telescopes, globes, anything that you can make by hand including looms, jewelry, leather, fabric, pottery and metal sets, cameras, science experiment sets, model building etc., etc. The kids will love you for it. And did I mention books?

Infant Development and College
Gadsden County Times – 8/13/15

Over the years a persistent problem keeps hitting the headlines, and that is the gross under-representation of minorities, especially African-Americans, in high-paying but extremely complex fields of study, such as engineering, physics, chemistry, etc. A lot of talk has been given to better college recruiting, better high school preparation, a better career counseling system as remedies, all of which are good ideas, but all of which focus on the older child. I believe that this focus on the older child, though understandable, causes many to miss some of the real causes of the problem, thus missing some of the real solutions. I propose that we focus on the infant.

I am not sure that most people understand the importance of brain development during the early childhood years, meaning from birth to three. These are unbelievably formative years, all of which take place before any formal schooling. The foundation for the ability to talk, to read, and to foster an innate math sense all takes place very early. How the brain uses information to make sense of the outside world, the pace of learning, and how much information can be absorbed and retained is all being formed early. A child's outlook on life, security or insecurity, positive or negative, violent or safe, are all developed early and has a direct impact on how the brain interacts with information that it is supposed to sort out.

I don't believe that race has anything to do with anything as far as under-representation in college, except that some minorities, especially African Americans, are over-represented when it comes to poverty, unemployment and underemployment. I believe that the effects of poverty on child-rearing has everything to do with the problem, and can be seen in any downtrodden community, from Indian reservations, to white rural poverty communities, to African Americans, etc. It is poverty that needs to be tackled head on so that many of the infants raised in stressed circumstances cannot just survive, but flourish.

What happens inside a family without financial resources? There is constant stress and the attendant negativity that goes along with it. Diets are often very poor, affecting proper brain development. The vocabulary that is heard and modeled has hundreds of words less variety, thousands of words less quantity and is often negative, compared to households of wealth. The parents often don't have a very good education and are unable to pass on what is intellectually needed to their child. Often poverty homes are anchored by a single parent, who is too exhausted by working at low-paying jobs to educate their child or even spend much quality time with them. There is often little reading by the adults for a child to model, reading time often replaced by hours and hours of television, which has a profound and negative effect on brain development. There is often a dearth of positive adult role models in large areas of poverty, which directly effects how a child views himself and his future. Every single person who has made it out of poverty to become a success has a tale of how some adult, somewhere, had faith in them and spent the time with them to help them to succeed. Many children don't have that.

Our society needs to be set up where good child-rearing becomes its number one priority, with greed taking a back seat, or even being thrown out of the car. Jobs should pay a living wage. Tax systems need to be set up that reward companies for creating decent jobs in a community, and penalize them for shipping jobs overseas. Tax systems need to reward two adults raising a child. Schools need to be set up for loads of positive experiences for children from stressed backgrounds. The school needs to have outreach programs to help stressed adults. I believe that every child in the tenth or eleventh grade should take a course in child rearing to show the many things that can be done in a home to help an infant develop to their highest potential, most of which costs absolutely no money. There should be a pool of money to bring in adult role models, like the engineers and chemists that we want so much, and expose children from poverty backgrounds to things that they would otherwise not see or even know exists. There are LOTS of things that our great society can do to facilitate success in all of its citizens, but the first step is to acknowledge that a lot of children's problems, especially those experienced in school, come not from the child or the teacher, but from an economic system that has left way too many of our children and their families in desperate straits while heaping huge rewards on way too few. We can do better.

INFANTS AND READING
TALLAHASSEE DEMOCRAT – 7/26/17
GADSDEN COUNTY TIMES – 7/20/17

A lot of young couples having their first child, besides being elated, are wracked with all kinds of doubts and fears about what to do with this precious little bundle, because they have never done this before, the child looks so helpless, and the responsibility is so large. I hear you. I don't know about the fear part, but I can deal with some of the doubt part, as in "What do I do to help my child grow up to succeed in school, succeed on the job, succeed in life?" Well, getting your child ready to succeed in school and beyond is easier than you think and doable by anybody, and I do mean anybody, if certain guidelines are followed. So, let's get started creating a little, teeny, brilliant thinking machine. (And have fun doing it, or else what is a child really for, anyway?)

The first thing to understand is the importance of the first three years of life on brain development. What happens in the first three years of a child's life has multiple times more impact on brain development than any other three year segment in a child's life. Parents, understand and take advantage of that. Use this to your advantage. Since reading is probably the single most powerful academic skill for a human, we will start there. From day one, when the bundle of joy, (or colicky crying mess – whatever) is plunked down beside mom or in the crib, pull out a book and read to it. It does not matter that the child has no neck control, can't focus on anything and doesn't have a clue about anything, really – just do it. Read to the child for a few minutes every single day of its life, until the child can read back to you. Then you can take turns. When read to from birth, magical things happen in a child's brain. First is the comfort of hearing a parent's soothing voice. Second is vocabulary development. A child unconsciously picks up vocabulary long before they are able to talk. The more variety of words and quantity of words that a child is exposed to early makes a world of difference later on in life. When a child is first developing, you don't have to read easy "children's" books to them – save those for when they are starting to develop an interest in reading. Read out loud any history or biography or how-to-repair the car books that you want. Read for yourself. The larger and more intricate vocabulary the better. When the child can actually understand what you are saying and is interested in the story itself, you can switch to the adventures of the crazy green frog. Third, is that reading is seen by the child as "normal." It is just what adults do. They eat, they sleep, they read. When the child is able to focus and has neck control, it will watch the parent in the act of reading. Reading will become habitual and just a natural part of the day. All children want to be adults and spend half of their time copying adult behavior, for the good or bad. If it is implanted in a child's mind from birth that part of being an adult means reading and enjoying books, the parent has just given their child an invaluable gift that can never be taken away. Reading will become a habit that is deeply ingrained, for life. The brain will also absorb the process of reading – how to hold the book, going from left to right, top to bottom. Once the child can sit in a parent's lap, they can interact with the parent and the book. The parent can point things out. The child begins to associate symbols – letters and letter groups – with sounds. The child will learn a couple of simple words. The child will eventually string a few words together and feel the flow of reading. The child will enjoy the experience of reading because it stimulates the brain on a high level, bringing deeper thought and more enjoyment than television. The child will in fact become a little teeny, brilliant thinking machine, minus the little teeny part. Job well done, parents.

Language and Reading
Gadsden County Times – 5/24/18

As research continues on how children learn how to read it becomes clearer and clearer that the foundation for reading is laid out in early childhood, from birth to three. The advice to read to your children early is good advice, but the most critical advice appears to be to talk to them, and I mean a lot. The platform from which readers are built is made from the amount and variety of language heard from day one.

Households are way, way, different. In some households an infant might hear "Let's go out on the veranda where the breeze is cool. We can listen to the cardinals chirp to one another. What a luxury time with our precious children is." In another household an infant might hear, "Shut up and sit still!! I said shut up! And look how stupid you are. You spilt milk all over the place! If you don't sit still I'll give you a spanking!"

The differences in households is played out when children hit school age and is most glaring when it comes to reading ability. If there is no vocabulary inside a child's head, you can tell them to sound out a word all you want to, but if they don't even know what that word is much less what it means, has in fact never heard it before, sounding it out is next to worthless.

I have said this before, but it is worth repeating. Studies show that children that come from wealthy, educated parents hear millions of more words -quantity – and thousands of more words – variety – and most of it positive in nature than in households under severe economic or emotional stress, which often go hand in hand. Many households are also single parent ones, compounding the problem. At the center of all of this sits an infant who has no control whatsoever over his surroundings. Which brings me to my main point: All children are gifts to humanity and all children bring their own potential for bettering this world. They all deserve a chance to be their best self when they grow up. Society needs them to be their best self when they reach adulthood. So, how to reach into households that aren't doing so well in the parenting and childrearing department and help that household give the children the language background needed to be successful in school – to be good readers. This is a tricky question. Nobody likes to be told what to do. Nobody wants government or some agency prying into people's homes. How to reach into a household and help the parents give the variety, quantity and positivity of language that every child needs to become a good reader and a successful adult? I believe that schools have a role, just different than what we are used to. Instead of just boring PTA meetings, schools should offer parenting classes to any parent enrolled in the school – "What to do in infancy to help your child succeed in school" and language acquisition would be part of it." Many parents are very young. The school should provide young parents with home visits from qualified teachers or social workers to model language and reading skills to infants, and the importance of each. Prek centers should offer parenting classes in how to teach children how to read from day one. All of this should be free. Communities and school systems could offer some kind of financial incentives for parents to spend their time learning how to teach their infants and children to read. To back it up even further, every high schooler should be taught specific parenting skills in language acquisition and early reading to make sure that they are prepared BEFORE they have children, so that their children can succeed in school. All of society benefits from children who come to school prepared for success instead of struggle. .Helping each child reach their full potential is what schools are for.

MANIPULATIVES VS. ELECTRONICS
GADSDEN COUNTY TIMES – 3/17/16

I had an eye-opening incident the other day which has serious ramifications for young children. I went into a big-box department store looking for a puzzle. I know this seems odd, but I am 63 and a lot of people of my generation grew up putting together puzzles, sometimes as an individual, other times as sort of a family or friend gabfest. Anyway, I was told that there were none. They didn't sell puzzles anymore. Somewhat taken aback, I looked, and sure enough, the puzzles had been replaced by electronic toys and gadgets. From a purely profit-motive point of view, this is understandable. From a child development point of view, this is shocking.

When a child is very young and just beginning to learn about the world around them, manipulatives - meaning things that a child can physically touch and handle – play a very important role in a child's understanding of their environment. They learn by physically interacting with that environment. Early learning is not symbolic, but physical – children learn by touching – which is why taking very young children into a store can be a very trying experience; especially if the merchandise is expensive. The seemingly simple act of doing a puzzle sets off several complicated areas of brain development, all of which are worth their weight in gold later on in life. When looking at a pile of pieces the brain is asked to create order out of chaos. The brain goes into chaos-organizing mode. Shape, size, color, context are all clues as to what goes where, and the child physically manipulates pieces accordingly in a constant series of trial and error. Every error gives the brain as much feedback as every success. Brain growth is dramatic and plays out in later years in better mathematical understanding of spatial relationships.

This is just a puzzle. When you look at other manipulatives, such as blocks, Legos, Lincoln Logs, etc. you have the added bonus of creativity thrown into the mix. There are further layers of manipulatives, such as paper, scissors, paints and clay for sculpting that teach their own lessons when used. The point is that children, especially young ones, should be physically interacting with their environment for maximum mental growth.

There is nothing wrong with electronics, per se. There are two things that need to be kept in mind, though. One is that the more time that a child spends in front of a screen, big or small, is less time that a child is spending in his physical environment, cut off from the lessons learned there. The other lesson, maybe even deeper, is that electronic devices also cut off direct human connection to other human beings, filtering human interactions through a device, instead of being face to face. This has implications that are just now being seriously studied, many of which are disturbing. It may be responsible, in part, for the rise of rudeness, coarseness and mean-spiritedness in our society, as we are being unconsciously cut off from one another. The gabfest part of doing a puzzle or building something together may turn out to be as important to the brain as the activity itself. I believe that the scientific term would be bonding. If I was a parent, I would not rush headlong into pushing my child into the electronic world, which corporations would love for you to do, because the profits are there. Let the child learn from and enjoy the world that we live in, and enjoy the goodness of being part of the human race.

Math in a Cup
Tallahassee Democrat – 6/28/17
Gadsden County Times – 6/8/17

Parents, to continue a child's intensive math instruction over the long summer so that they don't lose their skills, all you need is a cup. A measuring cup, to be exact. A measuring cup has more potential to teach a myriad of math skills than your home computer and, the last time I looked, is a whole lot cheaper. A couple of important educational principles come into play, here. One, is that hands-on learning, where the child actually manipulates things in the physical world, is deeper and faster than learning the same skill by looking at a two-dimensional screen or book. The act of physically interacting with one's environment brings many more senses into play for the brain to make sense of the world than simply sitting and staring. The other important educational principle is that what can be seemingly boring skills, such as manipulating fractions, for instance, becomes decidedly un-boring when coupled with a specific purpose instead of being taught in isolation. The skills are learned quicker, deeper and last longer.

Enough of educational theory, let's bake a cake! Or biscuits! Or a casserole! The cookbook, coupled with a measuring cup is a math-learning generating machine. (And its fun, which is the third pillar of educational learning.) We'll start with fractions. It soon becomes apparent that ¼ cup of salt is real different than ¾ cup of salt. (Throw out the biscuits, quick.) That adding a cup of water when only a half cup is asked for has consequences, also. (Throw out the casserole too, which has now become soup.) The child learns that, by being attentive and exacting with their measurements, things will turn out just fine. Confidence and pride in making a quality "product" has many benefits for the child, including a confidence in his math skills, which plays out big-time later on in life.

The more a child handles the measuring cup through repeated uses the deeper the understanding of fractions, until you have got what you want – a child with an internalized math sense. It becomes an integral part of the child, not just some useless intellectual exercise. I have seen this played out in real life over and over again when I trained ESE students for jobs at a vocational school. Whether it be auto mechanics or carpentry, you can tell when the young adult has, through repeated math use in a practical setting, crossed over the bridge from having to think about fractions to internalizing and "feeling it." Then you have a real professional on your hands.

Back to the measuring cup: opposite the fractions, you have ounces. Now you have entered a whole new ballgame that can be internalized, opening the door to pints and quarts, etc. You can also cross over back and forth between those two measuring worlds. (8 oz. is equal to one cup.) After the ounces, if you turn the measuring cup around, you will find milliliters, which opens an entirely different door– that of metrics. Whoa, Nelly! Now the child can calmly tell you that one cup is equal to 250 ml which is equal to 8 oz. and might even suggest that if you add maybe 10ml more salt to the recipe it might brighten up this dull casserole. (The sound you hear is not the blender, but the parent's brain spinning around trying to figure out what the child is talking about.) A cheaper way to use the measuring cup involves just water, which is the perfect summer play toy. Add a little food dye and you now have hours of entertainment. (Or education – whatever.) "Let's see – if you add ¼ cup of blue to ¼ cup of red, you have ½ cup of what?" When the child realizes that she has just created "purple" you will hear a shriek coming from the young scientist equivalent to that of Dr. Frankenstein's "It's alive!" Then hand the child a little notepad to write it down so they won't forget. Then say, "I wonder how you make orange?" and step slowly away from the mad scientist so as not to get wet.

Phonics, Games and Reading
Tallahassee Democrat – 7/20/16
Gadsden County Times – 7/7/16

I have found that the best way to teach a child to read is not get bogged down in phonics, spelling, grammar, tense – in other words all the rules of the ball game – but simply read out loud with them, have them touch words as they go, and read until a sentence is smooth. Then go on. This builds a large sight vocabulary, and establishes the rhythm of reading. If the majority of reading is just following rules, some children begin to view reading as work instead of fun, and you begin to lose them.

So, how do you teach all of these important rules without turning a child off? First, don't make it the central part of reading, and second, make a game out of it. Children love having fun and will rapidly learn things if the experience is pleasant, because the brain will absorb information at its optimum rate. That's what brains do. Following are some things that I've tried with children that work.

Word families: If I discover a sound that a child is having difficulty with, we will sit down and make a list of similar words. Qu is sometimes weird to a child, but with some thinking they can come up with quart, quiet, quick, quartz, qualm, quite, quirk, quilt, query, quarry, quote and quintuplet. As the list grows the children really start to get into it and it is amazing what comes out. GHT – light, bright, sight, might, fight, etc. CH – chew, champ, change, chow, chimp, chicken, chip, etc. A child's eyes grow in amazement as the list just keeps growing. They love it. Sometimes I had to drag them away to lunch.

Rhyming word race – see how many rhyming words children can come up with in two minutes. (Sometimes an entire blackboard.) Bill, pill, hill, mill, fill, quill, Phill, kill, sill etc. The excitement builds as the clock ticks.

Dictionary race. Write a word down and yell "Go!" During the frenzy of a child tearing through the dictionary you can see exactly what kind of reference skills they have and can work on weaknesses.

Play clerk . Have ten folders with names on them and the child is supposed to put them in alphabetical order and file them. Better yet, tell them the cranky boss is going to be here in five minutes and is in a "downsizing" mood. Or, even better, let them be the cranky boss and let them examine your slipshod files. I have found that the children love to be the boss looking for mistakes and this really heightens their skills when they not only have to be able to do something, but be knowledgeable enough to know when something is done wrong. I let them be "boss" or "bank teller" or "shop owner," whatever fits the skill. It is priceless to see the glee on a child's face as they call for the "security guard" in the bank because your deposit slip is so poorly filled out as to be incomprehensible. Then they have to explain to a sobbing and barely literate Mr. Hoatson how to fill it out properly. THIS IS WHERE THE DEEP LEARNING TAKES PLACE, when a child is able to explain to you how to do something.

Crossword puzzles: Age appropriate. Children and most adults love these things and they produce layers of invisible brain development just by doing them.

Lastly, pick three vowels and seven letters at random, like "A, E, U, B, M, S, R, G, C, T" and give the children 20 minutes to come up with as many words as they can using only those letters. The results will absolutely blow your mind, and theirs as well, once they see what they are capable of. The more they get the more excited they get, which is the whole point. If children are having fun using words, they are learning at a high rate and an adult can't ask for any better than that.

POSITIVE CHILD REARING THROUGH SCIENCE
TALLAHASSEE DEMOCRAT – 8/16/17
GADSDEN COUNTY TIMES – 7/27/17

There are some serious questions being asked in our society today that need some serious answers. "How do we lower the crime rate?" and "How do we increase the graduation rate?" are two biggies. The answer to both is simple: increased science experiments. What?!

We'll tackle the crime rate first. The more time that a parent spends quality time with their child, the more guidance there is to build character and intellect. Parents spending time with their children is a de-facto act of love. Many children in trouble at school or in the community are often in trouble because of a lack of guidance or care. Many children don't have enough adults in their lives that exert positive influences on them, for whatever reason. Many children are raised in single parent households, which can often mean that the parent is constantly working to make ends meet. Many children in America, where the average amount of screen watching (which is the highest in the world) is an astounding 8 hours per day, spend a huge chunk of their lives in front of electronic babysitters, in lieu of caring people. In the parlance of scientific jargon, this is "really, really, not good."

So, in order to combat the sense of alienation built up in children that don't feel connected to caring adults, a concerted effort needs to be made by each and every family to spend quality time with their children. This can include parents, grandparents, aunts, uncles, boyfriends and girlfriends. "Quality time" also means NO electronics, just real time interacting with the child.

The other problem mentioned earlier is how to create intelligent young people who will go on to graduate and become happy and productive citizens. To slay two problems with one stone, we are going to go with family science experiments. Parents, doing science experiments with your children is way beyond cool – it has all the elements of fun, wonder, creativity, excitement, education, adult/child bonding and did I mention fun? Also, this is blindingly simple.

I Googled "science experiments for kids" and what came up blew my mind. Here are some samples: "Tornado in a bottle." The classic "Vinegar and baking soda volcano." "Optical illusions – the "bending" straw and water." (You can call water H2O and spend an hour on that.) "Oil and water and why they don't mix." "How to make an egg float" (Add salt) "Chemical reaction to blow up balloons." (Save your breath.) "Static electricity – how to make your hair stand on end." "Make a rainbow." "Invisible ink for secret decoding." "Heating up air in a balloon – what happens?" "Make a lava lamp." "Magnets – how in the world do they do that?" "Make your own magnet." Glue + Borax + ? = crazy putty. Etc., etc. There are things for all different ages. I remember being a teenager and getting a kit to build my own radio.

There is absolutely no end to this and the amount of knowledge and understanding of the physical world that a child gets from the excitement of an experiment – watching and wondering about new things – is infinitely greater and deeper than sitting in what can sometimes be a boring classroom. And all of this fun and learning is happening in conjunction with an interested and caring adult who is willing to spend their precious time with a child. On a deep level the child understands the love that is being shown by the adult choosing to be with them instead of a million other things that they could be doing. This caring and educational time spent between child and adult is a game changer in a child's life and has invisible but profound positive effects on children as they grow older. Science experiments have shown this to be true. You may want to Google some of those, also.

Purposeful Children
Tallahassee Democrat – 4/11/18
Gadsden County Times – 8/31/17

"Why am I here?" is a profound philosophical question. On a more down to earth level, however, it is the question that runs through the head of every child in school at some time or another. It usually rears its head when the child starts struggling or failing and begins to feel pressured to do better. As the pressure builds and failure experiences accumulate the school atmosphere begins to take a dark turn and out it pops – "What the heck am I doing here?"- followed by fantasies of escape. This, actually, is a perfectly legitimate question and it is important for parents and teachers alike to realize how important it is for the child to have a legitimate answer rolling around in his head and heart somewhere. The negative consequences of a child hating the school experience are many, not the least being the siren lure of all angry children with failure backgrounds– crime, gangs, violence, hate, disrespect – you name it. The importance of a child having a higher purpose to sit in a classroom cannot be overstated. To draw an analogy to combat, if a soldier has in his mind that the reason for being on the front line is to preserve his home, family, country, government, democracy or freedom there is a good chance that he will stay and fight. If he is just a guy who stumbled upon the nightmare called war out in the woods, any sensible person would flee. What you don't want are school-age children fleeing the school. They have got to be given the mental and character tools to draw on when the going gets tough, so that they are resilient enough to stay and get an education.

In many respects, especially for children coming from backgrounds of poverty, a good education is their best hope for survival and a shot at a decent life later in adulthood. Parents instinctively understand this, so it starts with them. The parent can lay a foundation of higher purpose in a child by cultivating a sense of self-worth. Never use negative language to a child, even when angry. Something along the lines of "It doesn't really matter what you decide to do when you get older, just learn to do it well. Whether salesperson, or scientist, or police officer, you have a gift to offer this world and make this a better place. Learn to use your gifts well. This is why I am raising you and this is also the purpose for you to go to school and give it your best effort. Learn as much as you can, because everything that you learn will lead to your dreams coming true. Do your best – the world needs you to do your best," lays the groundwork for a positive self-image. When the child does something wrong, go to that positive self-image every time. "What in the world? Scientists don't do this. Police officers don't do this. I love you all day long, but I expect better from you, and so should you. Now, let's get on with being somebody important…"

Teachers, it is equally important that you carry on the parent's work and understand what purpose a student is carrying around in their head and use it in the classroom. As a child gets older, they may start to become more focused in their vision of adulthood. This makes it easier to gear math, English or science instruction specifically to that child's interests, which makes what can sometimes be boring subject matter relevant to the child's life. Relevancy makes learning infinitely more interesting, and interesting creates a student learning at optimum speed and retention. Knowing a child's positive self-purpose and self-image also helps with behavior problems, creating an avenue for discipline that is also positive and constructive in nature. Children will accept discipline much more readily if it is not seen as simply punitive, but is actually constructive and purposeful – to help the child achieve their greatness. In short, if parents and teachers work together to instill a positive purpose in a child's mind, it will work wonders for that child to be successful not only in school, but in adult life.

READING IS EVERYTHING
TALLAHASSEE DEMOCRAT – 6/11/16
GADSDEN COUNTY TIMES – 4/28/16

If there is one academic skill that rises above all others in importance, it is reading, especially in today's modern world. If a child can read well, which includes comprehension, they can teach themselves all kinds of things without outside help. Without the ability to read, one is lost in a literate society and becomes very dependent on others for almost everything. Reading is simply the power and freedom to control one's life, sorting through information to make sense of the outer world. Since reading is so important, it begs the question, what can be done to help insure that a child can read up to the maximum ability that their brain will allow? How do you foster reading ability?

Parents, these questions are directed directly at you, because a tremendous amount of brain development happens between birth and three years old. What happens in a child's mind before they are four years old can have an enormous impact, positive or negative, for the rest of the child's life. Besides being scary, the implications of this are that parents have a lot of influence over their child's future reading ability. This is good news, especially if the parent does a few simple, but critical things early in a child's life.

First of all, start early. I mean from week one type of early. Read to that child every single night, whether or not they understand anything or can hardly even focus their eyes yet. This puts reading front and center in a child's life, making reading as normal and natural as eating. It becomes as normal as speaking. Just as an infant's brain is hard-wired to make sense out of abstractness, such as language, repeated reading allows the brain to make sense of the printed page, including left to right, top to bottom, and eventually decoding the sounds that a letter makes corresponding to speech. And all of this is happening without the parent having to do any real "teaching." On top of this is the pure enjoyment gotten from the bonding time while reading.

The word "enjoyment" is critical here, and is probably the single most important component of teaching reading. Always, always, make the experience enjoyable. As the child gets older and is asking questions about letters and words, make sure that the child is having fun. Never try to force anything. It is counterproductive, like trying to force a child to speak before they are ready. Encouragement is great, demanding is not. If reading is a pleasant experience, the child will learn how to read quickly, because that is how the brain works. If reading becomes a chore, unpleasant or punitive, avoidance kicks in and the child will go "Huckleberry Finn" on you, escaping to a mental safe place.

Another way to foster reading is to make sure that books are a natural part of the household. Have them around, lots of them. They make cloth books for infants. They can chew on them and play with them while they try to "read" them. They make waterproof, plastic books for the bathtub. Keep books in the child's bedroom as well as around the house, so that books become a natural part of the child's life. Even better, give books as gifts and start early. When a child receives a book for a birthday, etc., it adds a special meaning to them. It raises the value of a book in the child's eyes because an adult is giving it to them. If an adult values books, the child will also.

This leads directly to modeling, which all parents do, like it or not. A child's biggest wish is to be an adult, and will copy whatever adult behavior they are surrounded by. This is not always a good thing, but can be if an adult intentionally models certain good behaviors – such as reading. As a parent, you don't have to constantly cluck your tongue about how important reading is; you just have to read. Read a book for at least fifteen minutes a day and have the child see you do it. If reading is part of your day, it will become part of their day.

Everything that I have said is really simple, but a parent has to be conscious of purposely creating reading ability in a child. Unfortunately, a lot of parents are overworked (and underpaid) and are exhausted, and fall into the trap of allowing TV to act as babysitter. Just always keep in mind that the first three years of life only come once, and if a parent is able to establish reading as an important part of life for that child, it will last that child a lifetime. It is one of the best gifts that any parent can give a child, and is open to anybody willing to take the time to do so. My praise and tip of the hat to parents, everywhere.

Reading vs. Television
Tallahassee Democrat – 8/3/16
Gadsden County Times – 8/4/16

A lot of children spend a tremendous amount of time watching television. American children watch by far and away more television than any other children in the world. There are also many, many children who don't spend much of their week reading an actual book. Now, I am not hating on television here, (I have one of my own), but it is very important that parents understand the effects of television vs. the effects of reading on brain development. Reading and watching TV are absolutely not an equivalent way for a child to spend their time.

I am going to start with two givens: That reading is the single most important academic skill that a child can possess and that a huge amount of brain development takes place in the first few years of life. Both have large ramifications for failure or success in the child's adulthood.

When a child reads a book several parts of the brain become very active. The child is decoding symbols and turning it into language. The child then turns that descriptive language into "pictures" inside their head, actually visualizing what the writer is saying. The better the writer, the better the visualization. The brain is also pulling meaning and understanding out of these symbols and as the vocabulary expands, deeper and more varied meaning and understanding becomes possible. There are dozens of parts of the brain that act in coordination to read well, and put all together is called "thinking."

The physical act of watching television is "anti-thinking." The TV is called the electronic fireplace for a reason. When one comes home from a hard day at work, the television often gets turned on. When you are watching television, all of those parts of the brain that go into overdrive when you are reading are put to sleep, and your brain gets to "relax" because there is little work to do. The TV electronically shoots images straight into the brain through the eyes. The brain doesn't have to decode, form pictures in the head, or even create any deep level of understanding. Every single brain function is done for it by the injection of the images into the head, so the brain goes into a state between consciousness and sleep, the exact same way that it did before TV when people would relax by staring into a fire or fireplace. There is absolutely nothing wrong with an adult turning one's brain off after working all day. What you don't want to do is use the TV as an "electronic babysitter" and turn a toddler's brain off, especially when that brain is wide open for real – life learning.

Too much TV watching can shorten a child's attention span. It takes patience and attention to read a book or study hard. Television is easy and quick gratification and rewires the brain to expect that.

The pacing of television is quick, often frenetic, and doesn't allow for deep thinking or introspection. Reading a book allows you to go back and reread, if need be, for better understanding. Watching television is different. Once an image is gone, it's gone, being replaced by another set of images, yet another, with no time or real way to dissect on a deep level what you are receiving. With a book, the pace and depth of what you receive is under your control, with TV it is in somebody else's control. This is why TV is such a powerful propaganda tool, for good or bad.

Parents, build your child for success, and build them early. Read to them every day and have them read to you when they are ready. Make reading one of the main entertainment vehicles in your household when there is downtime. Make reading fun and a natural part of each day. The simple act of reading wiil create brain development that will enable your child to think and understand deeply later on in life. Limit TV viewing. Let your child become the master of their own brain, not outside influences. When not reading, encourage the child to actually go outside and do something. Heaven forbid the TV gets dusty.

Reading, Children and Summer
Tallahassee Democrat – 6/13/18
Gadsden County Times – 6/7/18

Summer vacation is upon many children, which can be a blessing and a curse for them. I am going to talk specifically about reading here, because reading is probably the single most important academic skill that any child can have. Summer can be a blessing because for many children it provides the free time to actually read a book, which is a luxury that isn't usually indulged in during the school year because of the other reading and studying demands of the school. On the other hand summer can be a curse if a child has been turned off by the afore-mentioned reading and studying demands and they view summer as absolute freedom to avoid anything school-like, including reading a book. Especially reading a book.

This is the equivalent of a toned athlete deciding that once basketball season is over to chuck the whole thing and binge on donuts and Oreos while sitting and watching television or his teeny weeny ipad screen all day for months. The word toned no longer applies to the athlete. This analogy is more apt than you think, because this is exactly what a lot of children will do over the summer as well as not read. They are destroying both body and mind at the same time. Parents are running the gamut from not amused to appalled, and for good reason. What is happening to a lot of children is definitely not good.

Over the years fewer and fewer children and adults read books. The electronic monster in the room is sucking up more and more of a person's attention and time, which may involve some reading, but does not come near to the brain development that is caused by reading an entire book. The ability to concentrate, focus, have patience, form complex thoughts, build vocabulary, involve emotions, create over-arching understandings, form language, and create the excitement that comes from a brain being fully engaged and learning is what reading a book does. Losing the ability to sit and read an entire book is bad enough, but losing the desire to even try is worse. Summer is the perfect time for parents to work on a reading plan for their children.

The desire to read is the key. Start early. All little children want to read. Set aside a half an hour each day for reading, and then have reading at bedtime. If reading becomes a habit, it will stick, because reading is such an enjoyable exercise for the brain. Older children may have found reading to be drudge work, depending on what they are forced to read at school. If so, also set up a reading time during the day, but let them pick out the book. As long as they are enjoying reading, and as long as it is a real book, the benefits of enjoying the act of reading will pay off in dividends later on in life. Again, once the habit of reading is ingrained as a way of spending time, it will stick. Right now, if a child is asked what do they want to do during a long, boring day at the house, the idea of reading a book is about 28th on the list, right behind doing the dishes and mowing the lawn. If a child of any age is consistently exposed to reading enjoyable material their brain is automatically going to like it, just like the brain is excited by enjoyable music or the stomach by good food. If the ear hears nothing but an off key but really loud garage band or food consists of two year old soggy spinach in a can, then music and food will be avoided like the plague.

Schools should take a hint here. There should be enjoyable reading during the school day. I had the luxury of taking a literature class in high school and I could pick from a list of hundreds of books to read during class. The only rule was, you had to read for fifty minutes each day. I loved it. Everybody loved it. I still love reading. Parents, give your children a gift and set aside a specific amount of time each and every day that your child shall read, and help them when necessary. Give them a large list or take them to the library and let them choose their own books and then sit back and be amazed. Once the habit of reading sinks in, it can never be taken away. Ever. Your child will love you for it. Have a good summer.

Reading, Entertainment and Summer
Tallahassee Democrat – 5/17/17
Gadsden County Times – 5/4/17

With summer looming and the school year winding down I would like to impart two pearls of wisdom to parents about a child's reading ability and their continuous improvement, which can take a hit over a long summer of TV viewing, computer gazing, electronic game playing, just plain playing, or generally doing everything under the sun except, of course, reading. Keeping in mind that reading is the single most important intellectual skill that a child can possess to further their dreams as a productive adult, a two month layoff from reading is not a good idea. (It is also indicative of a larger problem, that reading is not an integral part of that child's life, summer or no summer.) The ability to read is just like playing a musical instrument – the more you practice, the better you get. No practice, not only no gain, but a real possibility of regression – of actually going backwards. "You don't use it, you lose it" as the saying goes. So, no reading over the summer means not just no growth for a young child's reading ability, but an actual loss of reading ability, which will have to be made up during the next school year, wasting everybody's time, teacher and student alike.

So, for continuous reading growth in a child, especially over the summer, here is pearl of wisdom number one: Don't EVER equate reading with school. Adults know that reading is not just for school, but if a child gets it into his head that reading is simply another of a series of tortures to get through the school day - that once the school day is over he is "free" from all school entanglements – that means to the child that they are "free" from the burden of reading, also. If a child has a negative view of school, or has difficulty reading and has bad experiences with his struggle, such as bad grades or scoldings, then that is exactly what reading is – a terrible burden. As with all things painful comes avoidance, and with avoidance comes a deterioration of skills, which creates more painful experiences which creates more avoidance. This is why long summers can be disastrous for children with a negative view of school – they will avoid reading like the plague because it is all bound up in their head with school. So, parents, decouple reading from school, immediately. It is a necessary tool to succeed in school, but reading and school are two separate things. What reading is, really, is high level entertainment. Better than any movie. Far better than any TV. The saying that "the book is better than the movie" is absolutely true, because a good book brings a depth to it that electronic media cannot emulate. For a child to view reading as high level entertainment, it needs to be so in the household way before a child is school age. If a child is reading and being read to on a regular basis since infancy, they will have years of reading under their belt, of viewing reading as fun and entertaining, long before schooling can sully the experience. As the child grows up, their view of reading as "high level entertainment" will last, separated from what can sometimes be arduous or boring "school reading." Children raised with books will reach for a good book over the summer as well as for the TV. This is hugely important – a child actually wanting to read, without being forced. This child will read for entertainment and information as an adult. Parents, start early, often, and have fun – those are the core rules of teaching reading. Once it is fun for a child, it will stay that way forever. The other thing that any parent can do is read, enjoy it, and have your child see you reading and enjoying. Parents can read with their children, or have a reading time when each is reading their own book. Family reading time built into the day is a gift that will last that child a lifetime. Adults are role models simply because all children want to be grown. If a parent wants their child to curse, then curse. If a parent wants a child to read, then read. Sometimes it is as simple as that. (2nd pearl of wisdom: monkey-see, monkey – do.)

Revisiting Homework
Tallahassee Democrat – 8/23/17
Gadsden County Times – 8/24/17

School systems in many counties are revisiting their policies on homework – not just how much and what kind, but if any. Many recent studies have thrown doubt on the value of mandatory homework itself. After listening to a litany of complaints from parents and students, whatever value there is in homework is also being weighed against its negative effects on families. What was once thought of as a fairly benign part of the school experience has now become controversial and it is a good time to see what a good homework policy would look like - one that works for both parents and students.

As the home life of many Americans change, the nature of homework itself must change. A snapshot of the typical American family is very different than it was sixty years ago. Between wave after wave of divorces, stagnant paychecks forcing parents into two jobs just to stay afloat, and the rise of single parent households, the stability of the family unit has been rocked. (Unfortunately, stability in a child's life, or a lack thereof, has serious ramifications on a child's performance in school.) In many households there is simply not a stay-at-home adult who provides the constant parental guidance that used to define family life. Time with one's own children has become more scarce and thus much more precious, now defined as "quality time." So, one of the biggest knocks against homework, especially hours of it per evening, is that it steals whatever "quality time" that many parents have with their children, thus wreaking havoc with any type of real flow in their home life.

One of the other negative effects of a lot of homework, is what if a child can't do it? And what if there is no one there to help them – either through a lack of ability or a lack of time? One thing that can happen is that a child learns a lot of bad habits that need to be undone the next day, because he made a lot of mistakes in his homework. Another thing that can happen is the firestorm of negative events that happens when there is too much stress in a household and the child is "failing" at homework and at school. Stress and punishment because of school will have dramatic negative consequences on a child as they get older.

So, what is a good homework model? Many European countries, such as the Swiss, have decided to give none at all. They feel that a child can only absorb so much in a day and that the downtime from school – known as family life – is not only important for the overall well-being of the child, but actually makes them better students when they are in the classroom, because they are not burned out. I recently read in a newspaper article that Marion County decided to cut out most homework (except for projects) but asks for a 30 minute reading session each night. I would like to suggest a hybrid that would fit each individual family's needs and schedule. Basically, no mandatory homework .I use the word mandatory on purpose, because parents themselves would be in charge of what was done each night. I think that each child could bring home samples of what they did during that day for the parents to look at. The parent simply signs that they have seen it. If the parent wishes to go over it with the child, fine. If the parent wants the child to do one or two items more to show competency, fine. The parent can control the amount of homework (or none) that fits his child. I also think that a 30 minute reading time each night is a really good idea. It can be anything that the child wishes to read and the parent simply signs saying that they did so. The act of reading and enjoying it each night works on brain development in many different ways and also counteracts a steady diet of electronic stimulation. It is important that any extension of the school into the household is pleasant and productive, just like school itself should be.

ROLE PLAY AND MAKE BELIEVE
TALLAHASSEE DEMOCRAT – 11/30/16
GADSDEN COUNTY TIMES – 11/17/16

If you have any of these clothing items and accessories, please drop them off at your nearest Headstart Center for three year olds: Sailor's hat, hard hat, surgical mask, tool belt, nurses cap, work boots, police hat, fireman's coat, uniform tops of any kind, stethoscope, lab coat, microscope, stuffed animals and dolls, cowboy boots, or anything else that comes to mind so that children can role model working adults. The list is endless and the more the merrier, because role-play is a powerful brain-building and character building tool. I was a teacher at a Headstart Center and had a role-play center full of different clothes that children had access to, daily. I got to watch the benefits of children being free to use their imaginations, which are multi-leveled. (One of the benefits for me was the chance to see what children actually think about adults, as they pretend to be one. As an eye-opener, have them pretend to play "Teacher," stand back, and see what you really look like. Having a sense of humor is a large plus here.)

Playing "make-believe" is a mental growth exercise that has extraordinary benefits for children. First of all, it allows the child to use their imagination to create a vision of themselves as an adult. The ability to imagine and pretend futures that don't exist yet is one of a human being's most unique and precious assets. Letting children exercise their imagination, just like an athlete exercises muscles, will pay dividends in the future in the real world, especially in the sciences. Things are changing so rapidly on this planet that many jobs and challenges don't even exist yet. Flexible and creative minds are going to be needed to meet them.

Grown-up role-play amongst small children helps them visualize themselves as productive adults doing positive, important and career-based things. This is good for all children, but especially good for those that come from harsh, stressed or barren backgrounds. Some children grow up in neighborhoods wracked by poverty or unemployment. Pretending to be a doctor taking care of patients, a veterinarian treating sick animals, or a mechanic repairing a race car allows a child to mentally escape the powerlessness of their environment and experience the powerfulness of the role that they are assuming. Children who are surrounded by struggling communities need to see beyond the struggle and see a bright future. If the school cannot help them do that physically, they can help the child do it mentally, in their own head. The earlier that children can see themselves as positive contributors to society, the better. A child's own self image drives the train.

Role play lets a child experience all kinds of jobs - a variety of adult roles - that they may wish to explore further as they get older. Some will feel right, some won't. That is why a large variety of clothes and accessories are important to have on hand, so that a child may shed many skins each week. A well-stocked wardrobe area in a classroom can expose children to possibilities for their future that many don't see in their surrounding environment, creating hopes and dreams in their mind that would not exist if not cultivated. Teachers can help guide constructive role play by introducing new clothing items and accessories with films, stories or actual career-based people talking to the children. Teachers can also carefully observe how a child acts as an adult and reinforce the positive aspects, while keeping an eye on the negative aspects, such as excessive hitting of the dolls, abusive language or mistreatment of the animals. Role play can be a mirror into a child's life and allows an observant teacher to try and help the child by reinforcing positive behavior and reshaping negative behavior. On top of all of this is the plain fact that role-playing is incredibly fun and entertaining , both for the child and adult. It makes TV pale in comparison, rivaled only by some of Shakespeare's better efforts. Grab a chair, raise the curtain!

Science in the Summer Stars – Gadsden County Times – 6/21/18

One of the main thrills for children on summer vacation is that they get to stay up later at night, instead of going to bed at sunset to be ready for school at sunrise. Parents, this is a perfect opportunity for an incredible amount of learning and it is simple: just wait until the night sky is real dark, take the children outside, and tell them to look up. You don't even have to say anything, because a child staring at the cosmos laid out in front of him will be awestruck at its beauty and vastness and latent meaning and the brain will undergo a wildly almost religious/spiritual experience. It happens automatically, and once it happens the parent can open their mouth and let the teaching begin.

The magic of the night sky is a gift to any child, but is not readily accessible to many. Light pollution is rampant in cities and there are millions of children that don't get the full effect of seeing the universe on a real dark and clear night because it is never real dark. Parents, make a concerted effort to give your child this experience and travel, if need be, somewhere out in the country and set up shop at night. This is what picnics are for.

The other reason that children don't see the night sky is because they are constantly bent over staring at their iphone. Looking up is unnatural. In this case, the phone is ok because it has an app on it called "sky map" where you simply aim the phone at the stars and it will identify the constellations, stars and planets. It is way cool. You can even aim the "sky map" at your feet and it will reveal the constellations that appear on the other side of the Earth. Let the games begin!

Before any teaching starts it is very valuable for the child to just soak in the experience of staring at the cosmos. It sets off a series of internal questions that mankind has been pondering for centuries and the very, unfathomable vastness of it all puts life on this planet in a very different perspective. The questions will come tumbling out from the child – "why, what, how, when, where?" and the scientific answers that a parent can provide doesn't erase the mystery of it all, it just deepens it, because the scientific reality of what is going on just makes one shake their head in disbelief, and I'm talking adults here.

"The stars are just like our sun – they are huge bright balls of burning gas which is why you can see them. Planets are like the Earth – they are not burning, so they don't put out its own light, so you can't see them from real far away. The closer ones, just like the moon, can sometimes be seen because the sunlight reflects off of them." So far, so good. The child can digest this. Now the child should fasten her mental seatbelt. "There are trillions of stars – more than all of the sand on all of the beaches of the Earth." ("What?") Around those stars revolve an unknown amount planets, some of which may have life, depending on the definition of "life." Even bacteria is a life form." "Light travels at 186,282 miles per second, or 670,616,629 miles per hour.)("What?!")"The universe is so vast that a new math had to be invented – many of those stars are light YEARS apart." (What?!?!) "The light you see coming from some stars may have been traveling for millions of years to reach your eye and the star may not even exist anymore." ("WHAT?!?!?!") As you approach the speed of light time slows down, so somehow time, space and speed are all interrelated. Einstein called in spacetime." ("Dad, have you been drinking?) Space is a vacuum, which is why you can see everything… There are black holes in different parts of the universe that act as a gigantic cosmic recycling machine…" ("Mom!!) "OK, let's talk some history – Romans and Greeks. See that set of stars there? That is called Orion's Belt. And there is his sword. He was a great hunter slain by Artemis in Greek mythology. Now, when the Chinese considered the stars…"

Sleep, Children and School Performance
Gadsden County Times – 3/1/18

The more I read about the stunning positive effects that a good night's sleep has on brain development in children and, conversely, the alarming negative effects that sleep deprivation can cause, I worry deeply about how many of our schools and pre-schools are set up. It is as if these studies don't even exist, their results being a complete non-factor in school planning. If the studies are noticed at all it is in the form of annoyance, because if they were heeded it would mean a drastic rethinking of the structure of the school day, which is one huge headache for everybody involved. It is easier to pretend that these studies didn't happen.

The NFL has had its "What in the world were they thinking?" moment when the seriousness of brain trauma was taken seriously, and it has started to change the game. As I watch school buses on the road at 6:00 in the morning and pre-school centers opening their doors earlier and earlier to accommodate working parents, I have the feeling that I am witnessing what will later become the educational system's "What were they thinking?" moment.

The benefits of a good night's sleep - let's call it on average eight hours- are many. Sleep acts as a brain detoxin, creating an abundance of good chemicals and cleansing the brain of bad ones. Sleep is where lessons learned during the day are cemented into memory. Even more than that, it is where the brain prepares itself for learning the next day.

What this means is that when a child doesn't get enough sleep, not only doesn't the brain retain information properly – up to 40% less than a well slept child, but the brain will process information more poorly the next day. If that child gets lousy sleep the next night, they lose a lot of what little they got during their stunted day. It is a vicious cycle made even more so by the fact that the bad chemicals that aren't cleansed out of the brain attack the sleep ability of the brain, speeding the downward spiral. Evidently some of these negative effects can't be reversed later on in life, can't be "made-up" by getting good sleep years later. And when I am using the word "children" I mean from birth through their early twenties. Some of these studies involved college students.

Just as in the NFL, dealing with a problem that goes to the very core of the game is, at best, really, really inconvenient. It is, in every sense of the word, a "Game-changer." In the case of schools, the entire game is education and learning and it is becoming increasingly clear that proper sleep is at the very core of the brain's learning process. Dealing with this realization is going to take some very creative thinking, but deal with it schools must. The fact is that schools don't exist in isolation, but when scheduling must factor in many outside forces including parents work schedules and proximity and distance from a school. And further behind the parents are societal forces at play that affect everything, including economic ones.

Somehow, someway, the school day needs to be structured to meet the needs of the child and not the reverse. Somehow, someway, the economic needs of our society should be set up to meet the needs of families, and not the reverse. The school schedule needs to be set up to allow proper sleep for children, thus ensuring that child has their best chance for a quality education, not just a rat race. School systems may want to embrace smaller, more local schools to avoid large bus times for children. This applies doubly to rural areas. The science of a child's brain performance is clear. Schools need to adapt. Please.

Summer Education and Home
Tallahassee Democrat – 6/7/17
Gadsden County Times – 6/1/17

School is out and the young children are at home. At home, as in all the time at home. What is a parent to do? On the one hand, most parents don't want to see the educational process stop just because it is summer. On the other hand, any parent can sympathize with a child's wish to forget about school for a while. For children who have had bad experiences with school, they would like it to be a looong while. Factor in the childhood lament of "I'm bored" with the parental lament of "You're wasting way too much time glued to the (fill in the blank – phone, TV, computer)" and what you have is, actually, a golden opportunity to further a child's education without the child even knowing it.

For starters, don't ever call it an educational opportunity or mention the word "school." Call it "neat stuff," or "way cool neat stuff."

Here is "neat stuff" number one. Buy a bunch of plastic, see-through cups. (When done, lessons in recycling will abound.) Get some potting soil and a variety of seeds that the child picks out – both flowers and vegetables. Place the seeds along the sides of the cup so that when the plant sprouts the child will be able to see every single thing that the plant is doing, including root and stem growth. Give the child a "job" to do – water the plants when needed and observe daily what they see. Now stand back and watch the child go nuts with excitement when things start happening.

The key to any real learning is excitement. The legendary Jane Goodall, who studied gorillas, remembers her mother letting her hide in the barn and observe the chickens. One day she ran out of the barn flushed with excitement: she had witnessed a chicken laying an egg. That excitement and curiosity lasted her a lifetime.

Excitement in a cup is going to go like this "Dad, look. The seed is opening!" "What are those white things?" (Roots) "Look at the roots grow. Why are they growing down?" (Looking for water. Anchoring and stabilizing the plant. Add words like "absorption.") "Look at the stem. It was growing down, but now it is turned up. Why?" (Looking for the sun.) "How does it know to do that?" (Beats me.) "Why does it need the sun?" "Why are the leaves green?" (Chlorophyll, food manufacturing.) Mom says that talking to the plants will help them grow better. Is she crazy? (They breathe in CO_2 and release O_2 – we actually chemically "talk" to each other.) "What?!! So, you've gone crazy too?"

Why, why, why, what, what, what, how, how, how? Education-wise it doesn't get much better than that. Now that the interest is there, parent, step it up. Buy a small "diary" and help the child record their observations, daily. A couple of sentences a day will do. Get them to pay attention to detail. Some of the roots look fuzzy. What are those "veins" in the leaf? Compare and contrast. How are the flowers and vegetables alike? How are they different? Look at the different leaf structure on different plants. What's up with that? Attention to detail is a valuable lesson all in and of itself. So is using the written word to organize and explain those details. Once the diary is rocking, go and get a paint set and paper. "Let's draw that flower. Let's draw that vegetable. What do you see? Pay attention to detail. Shape the leaves properly . Add the veins. Use a lot of brown for that plant – it looks like you forgot to water it." Painting adds a whole new, and fun, dimension to observation. And, speaking of forgetting to water – what happens when things go wrong? And why? Now you can go out to left field and experiment. " What happens if I add oil leaking from my car?" "Mom! Come get dad! I think he's going crazy again!"

Teacher and Parent Bonding
Gadsden County Times – 8/20/15

As the start of the new school year is almost here, I have a word of advice for both teachers and parents: become friends. Seriously. If not friends, at least come to know each other as human beings. This will ensure the success of a child in the classroom almost more than anything else that you can do. The easiest and quickest bonding time is from week one, before the child has had a chance to misbehave or struggle. The conversations are short, positive, and invaluable.

From the teachers, it would go something like this: "Hello, Mrs. Johnson. I am so happy to have Cheryl in my classroom. She seems like a wonderful child. She says that she wants to be a doctor when she gets older. I believe her and will do my best to get her there. I'll call you periodically and let you know how she's doing. You have a great day." "Click."

From the parent: "Hi, Mr. Hoatson. This is Mrs. Johnson, Cheryl's mom. Just letting you know how happy we are that you have got Cheryl this year. She seems to enjoy your class a lot. If there is anything that you need from us, please let me know. We're willing to do whatever it takes to help our girl succeed. It's good to know that she is in good hands. Have a blessed day." "Click."

Both phone calls took under a minute. Both phone calls also completely changed the dynamic in the classroom. The teacher's phone call did several positive and potentially important things for a child and household. Often a teacher doesn't know the dynamics inside a child's home. Each one is different. Some children come from homes that aren't doing so well. They can be filled with financial or emotional stress. There can be a fair amount of negativity in a stressed home, all passed down to the child. It may be headed by a single parent, who is just about overwhelmed by the burdens of life. It may be headed by a parent who didn't do well in school or has a negative viewpoint of school due to a series of bad phone calls about their child's behavior, which the parent is finding hard to control, or phone calls about academic failure. It is into homes such as these that the positive phone call becomes much more than a phone call. It is literally a life preserver thrown into a sea of hardship, and will be clutched onto gladly. I have had parents cry over the phone because they have never had a positive phone call from the school. They have never been told that their child is loved and appreciated. It is into these homes that are struggling that the positive phone calls do the most good and they should be poured into homes like these. Once a bond has been established between teacher and parent, the teacher is able to reach into that household and make positive changes. They can give solid advice on how to improve a child's academics or behavior and this advice will actually be heeded instead resisted because the parent feels that the teacher is actually on her side. The value of this bond cannot be overstated.

The parent's positive phone call to the teacher has much the same effect. Many teachers have had unpleasant experiences with angry parents. Many feel unappreciated and the enormity of the responsibility that they bear for the success or failure of so many children can be daunting even for experienced teachers. All are underpaid and overworked. All are laboring under sometimes ridiculous demands from several different government levels. Many feel like a soldier on a front line in a foreign country does: forgotten amid an endless war, in this case against illiteracy, ignorance and poverty. A good education is the only anti-dote, but many teachers are not feeling the respect that they should be receiving for fighting this fight. One positive phone call from the parent wipes away all of this just as the sun will dissipate the early morning fog. The teacher will feel like the parent is actually on their side.

Schools can foster the parent- teacher-administration-child bonding process. My advice here is don't have yawn-inducing meetings that bore everybody in the room. Hold barbeques and have teachers and parents bring food and sit around and eat, swap stories and laugh together. THEN bore them, if you must. Have the children perform something, ANYTHING. songs, drama, art shows, recitals, dance. (I find it amazing that all the stuff that parents love to see is being taken out of most schools. Go figure.)

If parents, teachers and administrators know each other and all feel that they are on the same team in the ball game of raising children, the chances for that child to succeed as an adult has just sky-rocketed. Now you've got a real school.

The Absolute Joy of Reading
Tallahassee Democrat – 7/6/16
Gadsden County Times – 6/30/16

I had an experience recently that I have had hundreds of times before, but the thrill never goes away. A child who I had been "tutoring" in reading turned to me excitedly and exclaimed, "Mr. Bill, I love reading!" Then, after some thought added, "I think that I might get an "A" next year." These two phrases were definitely not in this child's mind when I first showed up at mom's request, but now that I had heard them, I realized that my job was 90% done. The rest is just a matter of continual refinement of reading skills, or more simply put, reading a lot of cool stories.

There are millions of children out of school for the summer and there are also millions that aren't reading so well. The combination of the two is an opportunity for real growth in reading ability, including a sea-change in attitude, if reading is taught properly. If not done properly, however, sometimes deep-seated negative attitudes towards reading just get deeper seated, with more attitude. And, truth be told, a child's attitude towards reading is, as stated above, AT LEAST 90% of the ball game. If a positive attitude is internalized within the child, then the brain will naturally learn the skills at its optimum pace and efficiency. So, parents and tutors, here is a crash course in successful reading techniques.

Parents, you can do this all by yourself, but if an outside person is involved, whatever you do don't call them a "tutor." If a child has a negative view of school or reading in particular, the thought of spending their time over the summer being "tutored" in reading is enough to make them run for the air-sick bag. "Reading coach might work, or better yet, just "Mr. Bill is here to read about monsters today."

The first rule is "loving, kind, fun, laughter, clowning around and fun." It is a long rule, but it dissipates all of the stress that a child that is struggling carries deep inside them. Most reading problems are actually stress problems and bad experiences associated with reading, such as bad grades, pressure of being pushed too hard, being given tasks that they can't do, which leads to ridicule, which leads to shame.

The antidote to all of this is unrelenting praise when they are succeeding at what you are asking them to do. The first thing that you are going to do is ask them to read out loud to you. You have got to find their success level, where they can read most of the words, with a certain amount of smoothness. I usually bring books from all age levels with me, and we read until I get the right feel. It's sort of like the "Goldilocks" method, not too hard and not too easy. Then find a story at that level that is interesting to the child. Some old Disney stuff is great, but whatever. Then take it one sentence at a time.

Have the child read a sentence. Do not let them struggle too long sounding out unfamiliar words. Tell them what it is, repeat it and reread. Once they have mastered the sentence, have them read it until it is smooth. "Reading to smoothness" is important, because reading is like music, it has a rhythm, and once that child starts to read with that smooth "rhythm', they feel it and begin duplicating it. A child whose reading is very choppy needs to hear what real reading sounds like, so they read it, you read it back with smoothness and tone (Modeling – feel free to ham it up) and then they read it again. Once the child has mastered a few sentences, then have them reread the entire paragraph to smoothness. Once a child who has a history of struggling with reading can read entire paragraphs smoothly and correctly, you will see them light up like a 100 watt bulb. The "Aha, I can read " moment has arrived, the confidence soars, as well as the joy that goes with it.

What about phonics, you ask? Slip phonics in there, but don't make it the central issue. It completely slows up the reading flow. The child is building a sight word vocabulary through repetitive readings. After a paragraph is read well, then point out little items, like ph makes an "F" sound. When the child tells you that is crazy simply nod your head in agreement and tell him "wait until you hear about "tion."

When the story is done ask the child questions about it, pretend like you don't believe it, fold your arms and make him "prove it." When she goes back to the story and proves her answer correct, you know that she can both read and understand the material. It doesn't get any better than that. Have a great summer with your children.

The Gift of Reading
Tallahassee Democrat – 12/29/17

Since it is the gift-giving time of year I would like to suggest that parents, amongst the presents that are handed out, give their children the greatest present possible – the gift of reading. Not only is this possibly the best gift that a child will ever receive it is also the easiest and cheapest one to bestow. The holiday season is a perfect time to start, because children are home from school for an extended amount of time, allowing for some additional family time together. During the regular course of the year many families have parents who both work and family time together can be hard on a regular basis. Time spent with children can be doubly hard on single parents, especially those working two jobs to stay afloat. So, during the vacation days from school, when families get to spend a little more time together, is the perfect time to give the gift of reading to the little ones.

All a parent has to do is set up a reading time routine right before bedtime. The word routine is important, because when reading before bedtime becomes a natural part of a child's life, it sets off a natural chain of events in a child's brain that will lead to independent reading. The first thing that it does is unconsciously establish the fact that not only is reading special, but plays an important role in the household and in the child's life. This is reinforced nightly. What is also reinforced nightly is the love bond between parent and child as they get to spend some quality time together, which can be hard in this hectic world of ours. Nightly readings give the child something to look forward to each night. Children love bedtime stories, looking at the pictures and then back to the printed word, building a correlation between the two. This love of the story and the excitement that comes with it boosts the brain's desire to want to read to a high level. With a high level of desire comes maximum efficiency for the brain to absorb the mechanics of reading that they will observe on a nightly basis – that in America we read from left to right and top to bottom. That certain letters make certain sounds. That certain letter combinations make certain sounds. (Parents can have a good laugh with their child trying to explain why "ph" makes an "f" sound.) Slowly the sight word vocabulary is built, where the child will jump in when they see a word they recognize, such as "mom," "dad," "dog" or other words that have meaning in their lives, such as "unbelievably delicious chocolate cake."

Another important but subconscious thing that is happening is that the child is watching mom or dad read. This lets them know that reading is important to mom and dad, which sets off another series of events in the child's mind as they do what all children do – copy adult behavior the best they can, because all children want to be an adult. This aping of an adult's reading ability, if installed at a very early age, will pay huge dividends throughout the child's life long into adulthood. A child that comes from a house where reading is viewed as normal, expected, fun and interesting by the adult is light years ahead of a child as far as school ability, than a child that has no reading in their life, whose time is taken over by massive amounts of TV watching, instead. The holidays are the perfect time to give the gift of reading in households that don't already have an established reading time before bed. Just simply start doing it. If the child has gotten any books for any of the religious holidays (Holy days) start that very night while the excitement of getting a new book is there. New Years day is another good time to start a new routine. Books don't have to cost anything – frequent trips to the library open up a vast world of reading to any child. In case parents need any more incentive, doctors will tell you that for a child to get a good night's sleep they should stay away from electronic devices an hour before bedtime. Just read instead. Doctor's orders.

The Importance of Touching and Learning
Gadsden County Times – 11/10/16

How does a young child know what "three", or "3", means? The word or number are symbols that stand for the concept of three, but how does a child learn the concept itself? The understanding of what three is, or any number for that matter, happens in a child's head long before symbols are introduced to them. The concept of what numbers mean occurs through touching, feeling, and holding objects; manipulating the real, physical world.

Young children do a lot of their learning through touching and manipulating, which is why they are a disaster in an antique store. Very young children will go even farther and put almost anything in their mouth, which is why they are a danger almost anywhere and need to be watched like a hawk. Once they get past the phase of having to taste everything for information, they go to the touching phase. Children who are unsure of their numbers will actually count on their fingers by touching their mouth, thus hovering between phases. It is not until the real world has been touched enough and reinforced – "Yes, that's four napkins, very good"- that the symbolic world which adults live in with numbers and letters begins to make sense.

I am writing this out of the fear that many children are not allowed to dwell in the physical world long enough to really cement mathematical understandings and are being rushed headlong into the symbolic world before their brains are ready. The world and school itself are changing and some of these changes may not be good for children. One big difference is the take-over of spare time by television. Before the television era, children were naturally spending a lot more time in their physical environment interacting with it. They had to. Fast forward to the 21st century, and many children, even the very young ones, spend hours per day not interacting with their environment, but staring at a screen instead. Pile on top of this the fact that many parents work
g hours, or the phenomenon of the single parent home, making
ided interaction with the child rarer that it ever has been historically.
mply put, many children enter the school system behind where the

school system believes that they should be.

The problem with a child being perceived to be "behind" is that the remedy is often a rush to "catch them up" instead of actually slowing the train down and allowing the child to receive many of the experiences that he needs to catch up. Symbolic work sheets with numbers and words are pushed on the child and the child often struggles because the brain is not ready for the symbolic world yet. They need to be given the time to amass the experiences that they have missed, which is manipulating the real world. Instead of work books or television, the schools should spend their money on really cool manipulatives and give the child and teachers the time to use them until concrete understanding of numbers sinks in. "Hand me three cows, please. Very good. Now hand me two more. Thank you. Let's put those three cows and two cows together. Look at that. That's a lot of cows there. Whew. How many is that? No, we're not guessing, let's count. Touch each one for me, please. One, two, three, four, five. Excellent. Three plus two is what now? Five? Are you sure? Let's do that again." Yes, it is tedious and time consuming. Welcome to the world of the teacher. It is also vitally important that teacher and child are given the time to do this. Expand it. Group by fives – count by fives. Do it with tens. Multiply. Make three groups of four, or four groups of three. "Holy mackerel, they're both 12. Fascinating." The more a child physically manipulates items to solve math problems the more concrete and permanent is the learning. Do not rush through this phase. It makes the transition to symbols easy for the child.

The Library –
Vacation Spot of Florida
Tallahassee Democrat – 8/2/17

During the summer there is one place that should be every family's number one travel destination. It has everything that anybody could ever wish to see, has the lure of the excitement of the unknown, has a pleasant temperature and atmosphere and is absolutely free. No, it is not the beach, it is the library. The library as Florida's number one vacation spot is not as crazy as it sounds. Free public libraries are one of society's greatest democratic inventions, making them accessible to all. To parents that have never really taken their children to the local library, my advice is to do so, and often. The library has more to offer than you think and works on children's brain development and reading ability on several different levels. As a parent, you will be massively improving your child's mental capacity by doing nothing more than driving to an air-conditioned building on a hot summer day, which is about as easy and pleasant as it gets. And did I mention that it is free?

Brain building theory number one: Often children who say that they don't like to read say so because they are reacting to negative reading experiences at school. If a child's only experience with reading is to read what they are forced to – which they have no choice over – they can sometimes find it boring, uninteresting (to them), too hard or too easy. A child's view of the reading experience is more wrapped up in "I like it" than "I am good at it." This "I like it" part is hugely important, and is directly tied into a choice of their own reading material. (As an adult, just think about it this way – would you still say "I like watching television" if your only exposure to TV was hours on end of viewing the exciting "How to play the flute for beginners" program.)So, the first thing that a library offers is a vast variety of books, at all levels, that a child can choose from. It offers exposure and choice. The child doesn't have to read anything, if they don't want, they are learning just by looking at the titles and covers and choosing to read further into those that they find interesting. Parents, just turn your child loose in the children's section of the library and watch what happens. It's magic. They can easily spend an hour just flitting from book to book, like a butterfly from flower to flower. What is being pollinated is a constant stream of exploration, wonder, exposure, excitement and fun – all stretching the brain with new experiences. A lot of the "fun" part is because the child is in total control of the reading experience. "Enjoyable" and "fun" are key words for a child and reading ability. If the child enjoys the experience, (even if it just an infant chewing merrily on a cloth book), a child will gravitate to reading just as sure as a pencil falls when dropped. Their brain will also absorb the ability to read at its optimum learning speed because there is nothing negative for it to try and avoid. (Brain building theory number two.)

Parental involvement will rear its joyful head when the child starts asking questions – "What does this say?" "What is that word?" "Why is the lion so sad?" – pointing to a picture. "Well, I don't know. We'll have to read it to find out." Which brings us to more choices for the child to make: which books to actually take home and read? When a child says, in their outrage, "What do you mean I can only check out four books?" this is music to any parent's or teacher's ears. When a child is begging for more books, you have got them right where you want them. The answer is simple: "Well, we'll come back next week and get four more." And the next. And the next. Once going to the library, and reading itself, becomes a habit in a child's life, it will last a lifetime. Another gift is that this is child and parent bonding on steroids, especially if the child sees the parent enjoying their own part of the library. Parents, one last word on choice. Let them pick. Whatever. If they have a volume of "The Little Red Rooster" in one hand and "War and Peace" in the other, oh well. For whatever reason, they found them interesting. Enjoy.

Travel is Education
Tallahassee Democrat – 6/21/17
Gadsden County Times – 6/15/17

Summer is here and a lot of children are out of school with some free time on their hands. This affords parents a great opportunity to further their education and spend extra time with them, which is valuable all unto itself. Gas up the car and go someplace, anyplace, as long as it is different. The destination doesn't have to be far, expensive or necessarily historic or important.

Travel itself is education. Children experiencing some place new are learning on several different levels through all of their senses. As any Floridian can attest, one of the most memorable parts of first hitting the beach is not just the breathtaking view, but the smell of the ocean. The same is true with a hike deep into a forest. Sight and smell working together, then add the sounds – this is education at a deep level that cannot be reproduced in any classroom. Throw in touch – that of a starfish or moss or sand or a furry animal, and you have real school.

Different experiences flowing into a child's brain aren't quantifiable or testable, but are invaluable to build an understanding of the surrounding world. Planet earth is facing large problems, presenting large opportunities for those ready to figure out ways to make things better. In order to make things better, it is important to understand how things are now. Take them to the river. Take them to the beach. Take them to the forest. Take them to a farm. A lot of children think that clean water comes from a tap, food comes from a store and oxygen is just sort of there. Period. I remember going to a farm for the first time where I found myself standing in a pasture among a herd of cows on a foggy evening. I remember shucking corn for the corn roast.

If you don't want to go for the nature, go for the architecture. The old houses in Thomasville or St. Augustine have tales to tell. Pre-air conditioning houses teach us science. There are reasons for porches, tall ceilings and long hallways running through the middle. They teach us history. In Charleston, you can tell the union sympathizers from the confederates from the fences around the house. If they were iron, they were union, because the rebels had donated their iron to the cause. Rebel fences are wooden. Speaking of history, I remember visiting Gettysburg, gazing out over the peach orchard where Pickett made his charge and viewing the union hills ahead. It made the carnage of war very real to me. Closer to home is Andersonville, Ga. where the union prisoners were held. There are old forts to the east and west of us. FSU has a World War Two museum and FAMU one for civil rights.

If you like people, Ray Charles came out of Greenville, Fl. just on the other side of Monticello. Jesse Owens, who stuck it to Adolph Hitler and the Nazis during the Olympics, came out of Cairo, Ga. Or, if you like science, visit the mag-lab, or the marine-lab.

The point being is get in the car, load up some food and water, take the family and go, anywhere, just as long as it is some place different. Childhood memories will turn into adult understanding over time. This is a gift for any child. This is an education.

Wonder in the Unknown
Tallahassee Democrat – 7/12/17
Gadsden County Times – 7/6/17

For human beings, exploring unknown worlds is one of the most exhilarating things that they can do. The brain is literally on fire with excitement, using all of the sense organs to absorb all the information that it can when it comes across something totally foreign, totally new. Encountering the unknown creates a sense of wonder bordering on the magical. This is why people go to explore foreign countries, distant planets, the deep sea. This is why you should buy your child a magnifying glass. Say what!?

Yes, you can give the gift of wonderment of Lewis and Clark or Alan Shepard to your child for under ten dollars. You better buy two, because once you see how excited your child gets you are going to want to look, also. And once you look, you are going to want to completely hog the magnifying glass, leaving the child angry and frustrated. So, buy two.

What exactly is the big deal here? The big deal is that piece of glass on a stick is a direct window into the unknown. You may think you know things, but the magnifying glass gives you an entirely different, and exciting, view of even the most mundane things. This different view is learning and education on steroids. Your child will learn more science in five minutes looking through a magnifying glass than five hours in the classroom. And a child excited about learning and exploring is every teacher's dream – trust me on this one.

The child doesn't even have to go outside, or even get out of the chair, to begin with. Start with the hand. You can spend an hour looking at your hand under a magnifying glass. All the lines, the pores, the hairs, the unusual fingerprints, the underlying blood vessels – all bring a totally new and deeper perspective on how the human body functions. The added plus is that all of this new perspective turns a child into a question generating machine. Wait for it – "Why are some of my veins blue? I thought blood was red?" The child can spend another hour on the eye if dad will hold still long enough. The child will actually be able to see the tear come out of the duct when dad's team blows another one in the ninth inning.

Now the child goes outside. Bugs under a magnifying glass are endlessly fascinating, and I mean endlessly. "Honey, it's time to come inside, it's starting to get dark." "I don't care. Can I borrow the infra-red goggles?" When they exhaust exploring the thousands of bug species they can gravitate to the thousands of flower species. Shoot, even a blade of grass is fascinating when magnified. One of the huge benefits of a child examining magnified objects is their hyper-attention to detail that would otherwise be missed. This attention and appreciation of detail pays off big-time as they get older. It is what scientists are made of. There is another important, but hidden, advantage of a child exploring and interacting with their environment – it is a positive way of dealing the dangers that come with "dead time" or boredom. For the modern child the dangers of dealing with boredom are huge for brain development. Many children with time on their hands, like children out of school for the summer, tend to not know what to do and simply find ways to "kill" it. And to do this, they often plop themselves down in front of a TV or computer or phone, staring at a screen. Studies have shown the downside of too much television watching – everything from stunted reading ability and decreased attention span to obesity. Besides, "killing time" is neither learning nor living. Children need the tools to have fun and learn (two sides to the same coin) without electronics. This one is simple, get them a magnifying glass and turn them loose.

Contact Bill Hoaston at:
Billhoatson@yahoo.com or visit his website
www.childachievement.com

THE POWER OF NONVIOLENCE: HOW TO LIVE A SUCCESSFUL LIFE

PREFACE

Professor Johnson's lecture on the power of nonviolence was given at an In-House Suspension Room at Northville High School in the fall of 2005.

My name is Professor Johnson, and I would like to welcome you to our meeting of the "Might Makes Right Club." This is an O.K. meeting room, I suppose, but it's not nearly as fancy as the main headquarters. That one has bars in the windows. It seems to be an attention grabber, which evidently is needed, because the club members didn't pay any attention to the meetings held on campuses like this one.

Let me look at my index cards here for a couple of seconds. Is there a John Carter here? . . . Mr. Carter, I am going to make you club president. It says here that you decided to up the ante and use a weapon in your fight. Sort of "Even more might, makes more right." You exemplify the club spirit perfectly and now have a job title. What did you use, anyway? . . . . A brick? Was it your own, personal brick? . . . . Oh, you found it. Lucky you. Assault with a deadly weapon sounds much more important than simple battery. When you're in prison, don't tell them it was a brick, though. You'll get laughed at, lose your temper, and without your brick, what are you going to do?

May I see Latresha Shaw? Sweetheart, you are the treasurer. It seems that you are the only one in here with enough sense to fight for personal gain. As smart as you are, this was the best way that you could think of to get money? . . . . That makes sense. It is the quickest. They don't sell much at the prison shopping mall, however. Then there's always "Easy come, easy go." That fits in there somehow.

Who is Michael Brown? . . . . I see. It is written "I have a temper." Is that correct? . . . . Could I see it please? . . . . If I was a surgeon and could cut this temper out of you so that you could live a meaningful and constructive life, where would I begin cutting? . . . . It's there, but you don't know where. The main thing is you can't control it? Is that what I'm hearing? . . . . The judge is going to love that. "Yes, your honor, I have no control over myself. I am, in fact, a ticking time bomb, a menace to society, and I don't mean the movie. Can I go home now?" It all depends on the definition of the word "now." If that means thirty years, then yes. I have a temper. I love that. You better buy a leash for it. You are now the sergeant at arms. This will give you the opportunity to work with other behavioral challenged individuals who have lost their temper. Perhaps you can help them find it. It probably rolled up under their seat there, someplace.

I am happy to be here this morning, and I will tell you why. I can look into your eyes and tell that I am not dealing with crazy people. I am dealing with young men and women who are destined for greatness later on in life. I know it. I can feel it. I would not be here wasting my time if I felt otherwise. I am not dealing with crazy people OR stupid people. I AM dealing with people who have a near empty toolbox with which to solve their problems. At the end of the next two hours I hope to leave you with a toolbox that is fuller and more effective, one that you can carry with you for the rest of your life.

Let's open the toolbox that you carry with you now. Well, lookee here, it's not empty, like some of your teachers might say, but it has only one tool in it. Let's see what it is. It is, of course, the hammer. "Honey, would you fix the TV set, please?" No problem. Crash, crash, crash. "All fixed, dear." "The baby is crying. Could you put her to sleep, please." No problem. Crash, crash, crash. "She's asleep, dear." The hammer is great for some things, but not EVERYTHING. And if the only emotional tool that you have in your toolbox is anger and violence then you will not solve ANY of your problems.

The first lesson of today is VIOLENCE IS NOT A PROBLEM SOLVING TOOL. Let's examine that. Pick something to fight about. Yes? . . . . That's a good one. Girls. Frederick and Jeremy are madly in love with the same girl. We'll call her Bathsheba. What to do about this age old problem? How about beat each other to a bloody pulp? That's the ticket to her heart. So, Frederick and Jeremy call each other out and go at it right in the middle of the school, thus providing entertainment for the entire student body. These are not selfish young men. I'm rooting for Jeremy here, because Frederick is kind of a jerk and probably wouldn't treat Bathsheba right, anyway. What is the very BEST outcome for Jeremy? That he wins the fight, right? He is the man. He has sent Frederick to the hospital and thrashed a couple of his cousins too, so that Frederick won't get lonesome in the critical ward. Jeremy has now won the girl and would like to take her out but can't because the police are stuffing him into the police car. He does end up with a nice girlfriend in prison, though, but his name is Frank. Let's try the other scenario. What is the very WORST outcome for Jeremy? Jeremy wakes up in the hospital and looks like a plastic surgeon worked on him in reverse. He is now so ugly that he couldn't get a date anymore, with Bathsheba OR Frank.

At least both young men are still alive. What sometimes happens is the big, tearful, "I didn't mean it" scenario. Somebody is in the cemetery and the other has "I didn't mean it" tattooed on the inside of his brain until he finally joins his ex-friend. Did any of this solve Jeremy's problem? Of course not. While these two morons are fighting, Bathsheba ran off with Kelvin, who has his own car and has a steady stream of money, because he is employed.

Violence will NEVER solve your problem but is almost always guaranteed to compound it. Taking the violence road is the one way to insure that you'll never reach your destination. The strange part is that the people who insist upon taking that road are always shocked when they end up on some weird detour. "Wait a minute, this isn't Bathsheba's house. This looks like a courtroom. How did I get here?"

Let me digress for a minute. I was teaching my Sunday school class one day and I asked my students a question: Why be polite? I mean, really. Why expend all this energy going around being polite to people you don't even know or might not even like? It's a lot more fun being rude and a whole lot more entertaining. A whole television empire has been built on it. So, why be polite? This young man looked at me and said, "To get what you want." This blew my mind. The first thing that I thought of was, "Why didn't I think of that?" and the second was, "That is the most perfect definition of power I've ever heard of, THE ABILITY TO GET WHAT ONE WANTS."

Taking that definition, let's examine how to get REAL power, which is control over your life. Let's start with "please" and "thank you." . . . . What do you mean, "You're kidding?". These are two of the most powerful words in the English language. I can see by your laughter that you don't believe me. It's true . . . . So, you think that being polite is begging. And begging, of course, is beneath your dignity. You know, a lot of kids think like that. You're not alone on this one. I had a young man once who demanded that I turn on the air conditioner in class. "Mr. Johnson, turn on the air conditioner, it's hot in here!" I raised an eyebrow at his tone and agreed with him that it was indeed hot in the classroom. I went on teaching. "Didn't you hear me? I said it's hot in here!" "Yes, it is, as evidenced by the fact that I am sweating like a pig up here. Now, if you will ask me properly, I would be more than happy to turn on the air conditioner." I had my own dignity to think about. I continued teaching. One young man, thinking that he was being helpful, leaned forward and told him, "He wants you to say "please." "I know what he wants. I ain't begging for nobody. Begging days are gone." "What's up with that? Just tell the man "please." "Please?" "No way." Now the entire class started to get surly, because they realized that this guy would rather have everybody roast to death than do the right thing. I think it was "Tell the man "please" or else I'll wring your neck like a chicken" that finally turned the tide.

What on earth was that all about? I find myself asking that a lot these days, which is not a good sign for society. I also answer my own questions, living alone and all, which is probably not a good sign for my own mental health. But this is what I think. I think that a lot of students these days are overly anxious to be grown up, just like all the generations before them. And they resent being treated like a kid, who has about as much say over his life as I have over the orbit of the moon. From this point of view, politeness equals being weak, because it is just for kids, and rudeness and intimidation are seen as strength, because you are FORCING people to do your bidding. This makes a child feel powerful, or grown up. The problem is, while on this journey for respect, the student is holding the road map upside down and ends up wondering how he got lost in the woods someplace, because this rudeness thing NEVER WORKS and you end up spending every minute of the day butting heads with somebody because you are constantly making even the simplest things a battle of wills.

Let's start with respect, which is what all of this is about, anyway. You will never get respect by demanding it. You can produce fear, which a lot of people mistake for respect, but you will never get respect. You have to give respect to get respect. Try this when you get home tonight. "Mom, where's the food?" Scream "I'M HUNGRY, I WANT TO EAT NOW" at the top of your lungs and see if you get to eat immediately, not at all, or wear your meal on your head. At your first job interview, give this a shot: GIVE ME THE JOB BECAUSE I'LL

TURN YOUR CAR INTO A ROASTING MARSHMALLOW IF YOU DON'T." Let me know how your job goes. I mean the one folding the laundry at the county jail.

Young lady, could I please borrow your pencil for a second? . . . . Thank you. See how easy that was? And I now, in fact, have a pencil in my hand. I have turned my wishes into reality. I am a powerful person. Politeness is not for children. You teach it to children so that they know how to act as adults. Politeness is a social respect contract for all adults everywhere. It confers automatic respect between adults, including complete strangers. Instant respect. Give it, get it. If I say, "Thank you very much" after being handed food in the cafeteria I have just respected that woman for all the hard work she had done that day. If I say, "This food looks like diarrhea" I am now wearing a food hat again.

Since power is the ability to get what you want, the search for real power starts with respect. Self—respect and the respect for others. Everything is built on the foundation of respect. Which means, if we think about it, that power is an INTERNAL thing, something you carry inside of you. Those without any real power use an external power source such as a knife or gun, to make up for the lack of it. More on that later. Power is how you carry yourself. How you carry yourself directly effects how people react to you. You, in effect, set up your own reality around you by how you carry yourself. Let me glance at these cards again for a minute. It seems that a couple of you have developed quite a list of enemies in a very short time span. We've got two fights, three fights, two fights. Here's a good one, five fights. Mr. Rowley, I assume you are getting paid for this? . . . . Well, we need to have a talk with your guidance counselor, because fighting for free is a lousy career choice . . . . I see. It's that everybody hates you. I hear you. I remember my high school days well. I still occasionally wake up screaming in the middle of the night.

Let's talk about the law of Kharma. Anybody ever hear of that? I believe it's Hindu, and I believe that it is as real as the laws of gravity or inertia. Kharma?. . . . Very good. "What goes around, comes around." No truer words were ever spoken. How do they say the same thing in the Christian religion? There are several sayings to chose from.

. . . . "Live by the sword, die by the sword." Excellent. What else? . . . . "Do unto others." My personal favorite is "You reap what you sow." I believe that if you study any major religion, they all have a version of this law of REALITY. Let's do a little visual aid thing here. I'm going to write on the board three configurations. One is plus/plus, one is plus/minus and the last is minus/minus. There we go. The plus means happy, positive people, the minus meaning unhappy, negative people. Charles, come up here, please. Let's see what happens when two pluses meet. "Charles, how was the ball game last night? . . . . What do you mean, you didn't see it? This is pretend here . . . . That's great. I loved it too, especially the goal line stand. Great seeing you again. Take care, now."

Now let's try out the plus/minus. I'll let Charles be the minus on this one, which is usually a lot more fun, at least until you get punched in the face. We're walking down the hall and we accidently bump into each other. O.K., let's go. . . . . "Hey, watch where you're going you fool! You want a piece of me?" "I'm sorry, my bad. I was busy staring at Barbara walking to class." I go on, nothing happens. Now comes the real fun. We both get to be negative. Let's walk down the hall again. "Who are you bumping into, you fool?" "Fool is it? If you weren't such an epileptic, you could probably walk properly." "Why don't you shut up?" "Why don't you make me?" Now, this leads to the most famous Hindu saying of them all: "It takes two to Tango." Is there going to be a fight in this hallway today? Of course there is. Two thunder clouds have just met and there will be lightning. I am sure that neither Mr. Negative came to school to fight that day. "You reap what you sow." If you spend all day putting out negative, don't be startled when your harvest bears a bitter fruit as the philosopher The Shadow would say.

Those of you who are in constant conflict with others may want to do a little self-examination and look at what kind of kharma grid that you are putting out. Many young people these days watch a LOT of television and advertising. I worry about all those images showing men being hard, not smiling, the new ferocious man, like that is supposed to be attractive. If you walk around looking like that all day long, it's a wonder that you make it back from school alive each day. Just say to yourself, it's only TV, it's only TV. I mean, really. If you're in the grocery store and one cashier is smiling and waving at you to come through her line and the other one is snarling at an old lady because she isn't counting her change fast enough, which one are you going to go to?

There are three sources of power available to everyone. I'll write these down. You've got physical power, intellectual power, and character/spiritual power. Let's look at everybody's favorite number one go-to source, physical power. This is the brand "A" power source for five-year olds, because they haven't had the time yet to cultivate the others. If you are fifteen and this is still your brand "A" power source you are in deep trouble because brand "A" is no power source at all. It is the ILLUSION of power but is in fact a very seductive trap. You will end up powerless, whether in jail, in the hospital, in the cemetery, or if you're lucky, just sitting in a room on Saturday being bored out of your skull, while your friends are at the mall right now flirting with your boy and girlfriends.

Physical strength. I'll say one thing for it, it sure looks good. It sure feels good. Let's go back in time—It's 1846. You are a slave. Are you strong? . . . . I know you're white, use your imagination. Are you strong? . . . . Of course you are. That is what the man paid the big money for. Were there laws against weight lifting, against getting stronger? Of course not. Were you, in fact, powerful? . . . You were, were you? Are you kidding me? You are a SLAVE. Does somebody of color want to pick this one up? Would a dictionary help here? One of the definitions is, and I quote, "One who has lost all powers of resistance." I'll shorten that up for those of you with short sound—bite attention spans. "One who has lost all power." Go to any prison in America, and what are half of these guys doing all day long? Pumping iron. Working on their power source, like anybody cares. They are IN A CAGE, powerless to effect any kind of change in the real world. There were no laws against weight lifting in 1846, but I'll tell what laws they did have, to cut off the REAL power source. It was AGAINST THE LAW to teach slaves how to read. And this was not a misdemeanor, fifty dollar fine type of law. It was the hang you in the middle of the town square so that everybody in the county can see we mean it, type of law. Now we are talking about INTELLECTUAL power. If you go to a prison, the only one that strikes any fear into anybody's heart is the guy who spends all his time in the library. THAT is the guy to watch out for. The entire idea of a police officer having to read you your rights, the Miranda ruling, was hatched out of the head of an angry prisoner who could also read well. Look at our entire economic system. Hercules could carry boulders from point "A" to point "B" for an entire hour and have four dollars to show for it, after taxes.

Physical strength, by and of itself, is just about worthless as a power source. It does make you look cool in a bathing suit, however. The only time that it seems like a good idea to go there is in an attempt to get your way through violence or intimidation, which is mental violence. Once you go there, however, you have completely shut down your two real power sources, intellect and character.

I don't know how to break this to you, but fighting isn't what it used to be. Unfortunately, every teenager in the world has a brain defect that clouds the judgement. It is the unyielding belief that they are invincible. Every last child that I have counseled for fighting has taken offense to the notion that they might actually have something happen to them that isn't quite TV-like. They don't take offense to the suggestion that fighting is wrong, or that hurting other people is wrong or that embarrassing their entire family is wrong, but they will get downright angry if it is suggested that they are a mortal human being; are, in fact, a member of the human race. That doesn't sit well with them, at all. They are willing to fight all over again, just to prove their point, which is that they are living in La-La land and are perfectly happy there and are unhappy living here on Earth.

Mr. Randolph, would you please come up here and give us a demonstration of what a human fighting machine can do. Now, keep in mind that I am a defenseless old man, so everything we do will be in slow motion. And pretend. That pretend part is important. O.K., you stand over there and we will get into a fight over something significant, like a girl said that you said that her boyfriend said bad things about her. Here we go. What is the first thing you do? . . . . Oh, come on now. Everybody knows it's take off your shirt. What are you laughing for? You know I'm right. I would like for somebody to explain to me why they do that. I mean, you are putting yourself in the position of getting beat to a pulp and looking like Ygor for the rest of your life and you are worried about if you are going to have a clean shirt to wear to the hospital? . . . . That's alright, you don't have to explain it. It makes perfect sense to me. Right up there with this invincible thing. Let's go, off with the shirt, in slow motion. Now, when his shirt reaches right about here, is when I pull my gun out and BANG! Now I start dancing around like Ali, because this fight is over. NEXT!

Your main problem is, you're not insane. You are a normal guy getting caught up in something stupid. Not everyone one is normal. In a fight you've got crazy, crazier and craziest. Which one is going to win? Except you can't use the word "win", because the crazier you are, the more jail time you get. The last time I went to a real bar-Hooters doesn't count—was a long time ago. I saw two guys who both had minus signs all over them discover each other, which they always seem to do, using their hate radar I presume, and they started to go at it. I left around the time that the less crazy of the two was getting his nose bit off.

I love all of you in this room. I don't ever want to open up my newspaper and read anything about you but your graduation notice. You need to respect yourself and don't put yourself in dangerous positions. It is not a sign of cowardice, it is a sign of intelligence, which is the power source that you need to go to every once in a while. Even superman has to watch out for kryptonite.

A word on weapons here. There are a LOT of powerless people these days who want to be the man, and don't really know how to do it. With so many boys being raised in fatherless families, it's kind of hard to figure out how to do it. For only a few dollars you can buy at least a pretend manhood, just stick a gun in your pocket. The power surge you get is enormous. I can stick a gun in a baby's diaper and he will start crawling around like John Wayne. If you look closely, however, he still drools and cries at the drop of a hat and is no closer to manhood than before he added the two pounds of metal. It is the illusion of power that makes a gun especially dangerous, because the reality is the exact opposite. I was listening to National Public Radio once and heard an interview with an ex-gang leader from New York City, and he explained why he was on a one-man mission to get rid of guns. When he carried one, he found himself heading into crazy, dangerous situations instead of doing what normal people do, which is run for their life. The gun made him a trouble magnet. It also has the opposite effect of protecting yourself. It, in fact, makes you a human bull's-eye. You end up finding yourself in places you shouldn't be, yelling at people that you shouldn't be yelling at and then wondering why every night is a replay of the O.K. Corral. Do you know why nobody on the planet hates the Swiss? It's because they don't have a giant arsenal that threatens the existence of life on the planet earth. If they come unhinged, what's the worst that could happen? They close their ski-resorts?

A gun in your pocket screams to be used, just like money. Ever see a little kid with ten dollars that wasn't begging to spend it? On ANYTHING? "Please, dad, let me buy that necktie. It's a nice one." "NO. Save your money for something you really want." "O. K. How about this blender?" You are going to find yourself making up any excuse in this world to shoot the gun, or at least wave it around, because what good is your only claim on manhood if nobody knows that you have got it?

I suppose that makes a girl's claim to womanhood the razor. If a girl starts reaching for her shoe in the middle of a fight, it is probably not to tie up the dangling shoelace. Getting into an argument with another girl over somebody's boyfriend, who is probably cheating on the both of them in the first place, and walking away looking like a jack-o-lantern for the rest of your life is not going to land the guy of your dreams, unless he's Freddie Kruger.

VIOLENCE IS THE ENEMY. Violence itself. Not you. Not the person you're having a dispute with. Violence as a problem-solving tool. Don't EVER make the mistake of thinking that you are its master. That you can control it. History is littered with fools that think that they could control violence. How about a little slap-fest called, and I'm not making this up, the HUNDRED YEARS WAR. I wonder if they planned it that way? All this foolishness bankrupted the French, which led to the French Revolution, which is the poster child for violence run amuck. Off with their heads. Which heads? Well, after awhile, ANY head will do. The beast must be fed.

Hatfields and the McCoys. Well, let's put our families in the history books by shooting at each other FOR GENERATIONS because of a dispute OVER A PIG. Brilliant move.

The fact that violence is its own living, breathing entity which springs to life through the minds of people that have few problem-solving skills is actually incased in law. In 1926 Clarence Darrow, probably the greatest defense attorney that ever lived, defended a black man named Dr. Sweet who had moved into an all-white neighborhood in Detroit. A white mob formed outside the house for several days. One of the members of the Sweet family fired shots through the window at the mob killing one man and wounding another. Eleven black people in the house were arrested for first degree murder. Clarence Darrow won the case, even though no shots were fired first from the white mob, because a mob HAS A LIFE OF ITS OWN. VIOLENCE has a life of its own. It is the fear of that underlying threat of violence that allowed Dr. Sweet to be acquitted. I remember when I was in junior high school. I was talking with a guy that was a friend of mine and, for whatever reason, we started arguing about something. Other kids started gathering around and before I knew it, the crowd was taking sides and pumping up a fight. To my shame, I pushed the young man and he pushed me back. You could feel the hate engine being revved up. We looked at each other, fists balled up. I then looked at the mob around me and then back at my friend. I got mad at being put in this situation, where there was no real graceful way out. Fortunately, I was madder at the jerks around me than at my friend and I pushed myself through the crowd and went to class. I was fully prepared to spend the rest of my day in abject humiliation, but it didn't turn out that way. The crowd pretty much gave a collective, "Oh, well, no entertainment today," and went on about their way. My friend was just as relieved as I was that nothing stupid had happened and we laughed at what boneheads we were later on. I will never forget what the rising of the violence beast felt like, however. I was just very lucky that it didn't get fed that day.

Since violence itself is the enemy, what are we going to do about it? The human race, which seems hardwired for all kinds of vicious insanity, has been grappling with this one for eons. I am fixing to load your toolbox with some other tools to reach for besides the hammer. First, a little more history. There are a few great people down through the ages who became great by tackling this issue head on. A theory of nonviolence as a powerful problem-solving tool has been developed, used and perfected by Dr. Martin Luther King, Jr. to change the entire course of United States history for the better. Understanding what he did and how he did it will change your life, because it goes to the real meaning and source of power. To get to Martin Luther King, Jr., however, we have to go through three other gentlemen first . . . . So, you think this is boring? Are you kidding me? We get to talk about people getting tacked up to trees, being thrown in jail, beaten and shot. You'd sleep through an earthquake, wouldn't you? I will make it brief, however, because I realize that the mall is calling your name.

We are going to discuss four weak, sissy crybabies who also happen to be the most powerful men on earth. What separates them from everybody else is that they discovered the seemingly bizarre notion that love is more powerful than hate. Not nicer, MORE POWERFUL. They harnessed this love force to change the world. Now, since everybody's vision of manhood is wrapped up in being harder than an industrial diamond, this is all going to seem very weird. AT FIRST. Hang with me here. I'm going to show you what manhood is all about, never mind the fact that half of these guys seem to be dressed in diapers, and one's a hippie lunatic.

You can start your eyes rolling here, because I am going to give you a quick, HISTORICAL perspective of Jesus Christ. This is not church here and there are dozens of way cool religions that profess many of the same values, but to understand people like REVEREND Dr. Martin Luther King, Jr. you need to understand what Jesus Christ brings to the table, because in many ways it was a turning point for a slice of mankind.

The Old Testament, of which I'm sure you're all intimately familiar, is filled with violence, depravity and revenge. That's because Christ is nowhere to be found in it. The bible double clutches and throws itself into reverse in the New Testament, with the introduction of Jesus, who is the living embodiment of the love force. When asked what was the single most important thing that God expects of humans, he responded with, "Love thy neighbor." Asked to distill it even further, since evidently this was a little murky, he implied that God is LOVE.

Period. This came as an awful shock to the system, since this seemed to go against the grain of what humans are all about, which is violence, depravity and revenge. They knew that he was insane when he was asked what to do about violence, and he responded with "Turn the other cheek." So they did what any self respecting human would do when faced with insanity, they tacked his cheek and everything else to a tree.

Fast forward to 1846. Now you've got the grandfather of all hippies, Henry David Thoreau, who is thinking all kinds of crazy thoughts. This happens when you live all by yourself in the woods in a house of your own making, for years. WAY too much time to think. They didn't have all these electronic gadgets back then to steadily bombard the brain with SOMETHING, ANYTHING, to wash away the deadly silence, which is the birthplace of thought. So this guy's brain is in overdrive and he actually thinks that war and violence are WRONG, and he is not going to support a government that thinks that war and violence are good foreign policy, so he totally loses his mind and refuses to pay his taxes. Fortunately for him, humans had evolved beyond the tree-tacking stage into the much more humane put-'em-in-a-cage-until-they-rot stage.

Besides being a crusty old hermit, he was a brilliant writer. I am going to quote briefly from his treatise "On the DUTY of Civil Disobedience," which is the virtual constitution of the power through nonviolence movement. "A common and natural result of an undue respect for law is, that you may see a file of soldiers, colonel, captain, corporal, privates, powder-monkeys and all, marching in admirable order over hill and dale to the wars, against their wills, aye, against their common sense and consciences, which makes it very steep marching indeed, and produces a palpitation of the heart. They have no doubt that it is a damnable business in which they are concerned; they are all peaceably inclined. Now what are they? Men at all?" * . . . . I'll continue farther on. "The mass of men serve the state thus, not as men mainly, but as machines, with their bodies . . . . In most cases there is no exercise whatever of the judgement or of the moral sense; but they put themselves on a level with earth and wood and stones; and wooden men can perhaps be manufactured that will serve the purpose as well.

Such command no more respect than men of straw or a lump of dirt." Holy mackerel! No wonder they put this guy in jail. He was a truly dangerous man. I bet you never heard anything like that on television. Corporations are not overly eager to have their logos identified with dangerous ideas. Bad for business. If you don't do anything else, you students need to learn how to read and read well.

The man is dangerous because he is powerful. His ideas have the ability to effect real change in the world. His power comes from his intellectual ability, his ability to coherently express his thoughts, and then doubles by combining with the third power source, that of character.

* Footnote—Henry David Thoreau, Civil Disobedience, published by The American Liberty, New York, 1960: 20th Printing, pgs. 223-224. Ibid

What was he saying? One thing he did was redefine manhood. His definition does not include physical strength, but the strength of DOING THE RIGHT THING, NO MATTER WHAT ANYBODY ELSE THINKS, AND NO MATTER WHAT THE COST. The next thing he did was define violence as unnatural, unmanly and wrong. The sounds you hear are the far-away echoes of Jesus Christ. And what got him stuffed in a jail was the gall to suggest that you weren't any kind of a man who could look himself in the mirror in the morning without retching at the coward that was staring back at you unless you did what you could to STOP the violence. Which, in a perverse kind of way meant that if you were involved in violence and you knew that it is wrong YOU WERE THE COWARD. Violence is an act of cowardice. Walking away is not. Now we are going to have a moment of silence here while we let that little brain blow sink in.

And the thing is, I know it's true and so do you. It was much easier for me to push my friend than to say in front of everybody that what was happening was wrong. MUCH easier, which is why I did it. I was in fact a COWARD at the time, because I would rather hurt somebody than face the scorn of my peers. I have seen kids lie, cheat, steal, assault and murder because they were afraid not to. Afraid of what somebody might say. Afraid to stand up to the bully, because then he may turn his bully butt on you. I hear you. Welcome to the human race.

Fast forward a hundred years or so, and we meet a gentleman who was confronted with a problem. He was living in India, a country that had been taken over by the British Empire, the most powerful empire the planet had ever seen. Just ask them, they'll tell you. His name was Mahatma Ghandi. He looked like he had a birth weight of nine ounces and dressed like it for the rest of his life. How you attract women older than two wearing a diaper, I don't know, but he had more pressing things on his mind, like bringing an empire to its knees, by himself. Force wasn't an option. The Empire wrote the book on the use of force. How about read a book and get some wild ideas into your head? He studied Thoreau and realized that this nonviolent civil disobedience thing might just work if you could find a few million people crazy enough to go along with you. This is where the character thing comes in, because you can't even get more than two people to agree on what to eat for lunch unless they have faith in YOU. People of intellect and character have figured out what drives people with intellect and no character: MONEY. If money is somebody's sole motivation for getting up in the morning, then you've got them right where you want them. Choke off that money supply, nonviolently, and it is amazing how all of a sudden you are now dealing with somebody full of character, willing to do the right thing. Just turn the money faucet back on. Quickly, please. They don't CARE if the money comes from right or wrong, so force them to do it the right way, and make it impossible to do it the wrong way. They're still happy, and you've got your freedom. Ghandi got millions of people to boycott British goods, taught people to make their own clothes, got salt from the sea, WHATEVER, just so you didn't pay the British for anything. If he had taken up arms against the British, India might still be a member of the empire, with its citizens drinking tea at twelve while doing their best to ignore the explosions and the occasional mass murder. The moral of this story is that NONVIOLENCE works to get your way and violence DOESN'T. To finish beating this dead horse, I am going to end with Dr. Martin Luther King Jr., for whom everybody in this country owes an everlasting debt. He is literally the founding father of modern, relatively conflict-free, America. Before I discuss what happened at Birmingham, however, I am going to give you a little visual aid on the power of nonviolence.

Mr. Randolph, my slow-motion fighting machine, could you please come back up here for a minute? . . . . No, I'm not going to shoot you in the stomach again. Besides, you've been sitting too long, anyway. O.K., here we go again. But this time, I am going to defend myself with judo. Come back here. I will pretend if you will pretend. Now, does anybody know what judo is? . . . . No, that's karate, where you actually get to hit somebody. Judo is the art of self—defense ONLY. No hitting. It is also a philosophy in which you use your aggressor's violence against himself, or herself, if your date has gone sour on you. Alright, throw the punch. You notice how I avoid the blow, take his arm like so, and by moving my hip I can throw him clean up against the wall? The beauty of it is that the harder he tries to hit me, the farther I can throw him. I use his own violence as a weapon against him. The crazier he gets, the more he gets hurt. Keep this in mind, because now

I am going to talk about Birmingham. Thank you, Mr. Randolph. You can peel yourself off the wall and have a seat now.

The Civil Rights march on Birmingham was a watershed in American history. You had hundreds of protesters in full Martin Luther King, Jr. mode, singing and praying. Not a gun, knife or fingernail clipper in sight. Singing and praying. Martin Luther King Jr. made a huge point of this. He trained people for moments like this, because turning the other cheek absolutely does not come naturally or easily. He knew that if there was any violence on THEIR PART that the entire battle for real democracy in the United States would be lost. What was waiting for these peaceful people was a butt whipping of gigantic proportions and it was not going to be pretty, WHICH WAS THE POINT. On television the entire country was treated to the spectacle of men, women and children being attacked by police dogs, beaten with clubs and the old stand-by, thrown in jail. In that short time frame, however, the worm began to turn. Judo on a mass scale was being performed to a world-wide audience. The violence, which was so near and dear to the racists, was used against them. All over America, while people were watching the nightly news, you had conversations like this: "I don't know Elmer, that don't look quite right to me. I mean, I might be a stone cold racist with a heart the size of a shriveled lima bean but whipping up on somebody's grandmother just don't seem fair. At least turn off the water cannon and let her stand up and try to get a couple of licks in." The violence was so ugly compared to the nonviolence that the civil rights movement was able to eventually throw that part of America against the wall, so to speak. And you, personally, may want to keep somewhere in the back of your mind that fighting makes you look like Peter the Pinhead the next time you want to beat up on somebody.

As an aside, sometimes you find yourself shaking your head. The only evidence I see for evolution NOT being true is that chimpanzees and apes don't go on rampages whenever they can't get their way, unlike us highly developed and evidently high-strung humans.

On a personal note, it amazes me that to this very day that there are some people who regard Martin Luther King Jr. as being weak. This usually comes from the "Violence is a good idea" crowd. Well, King had a very strong gut feeling that he wasn't going to be coming back from his trip to Memphis, but felt that it was his duty to go ANYWAY. If that is not the definition of manhood, I don't know what is. Gary Cooper got an academy award for it in High Noon.

Since violence is the last refuge of the powerless trying desperately to make themselves heard, how do you go about becoming really, truly, powerful? How can you get your way in life? I am going to use a four letter word here, which I don't normally do, but it is WORK. You have to work at it. Most violent people are simply lazy. They are going to take the shortest route possible to success city, except that they never reach the city gates. And again, this always seems to come as a surprise to them.

If fighting is not going to get you anyplace, what should you WORK at that will? Start with your intellect. Your brain. There is money in them there squiggles. Lots of it. Read, write, explore math. If a class is boring, get over it. Tape a twenty-dollar bill to the top of your desk to remind you of why you are being bored. People will pay you wheel barrels full of money to do things that they can't. I have got to pay some joker forty dollars an hour to work on my car, because I don't even know what I'm looking at anymore when I stare helplessly under the hood. I shell out over two hundred dollars an hour to have some lady tell me to calm down, because it's a pimple and not skin cancer. When I'm ready to pitch my computer out into the backyard I pay good money for somebody to talk me out of it. A huge part of the reason why you are in this room today is not because you're stupid, but you have no faith in yourself. You have no self-respect. You don't think that you have the ability to make money using your brain. SURE YOU DO. I have a picture on my wall of a young Hispanic lady. She is standing next to a large, double prop airplane. During World War II she would fly the plane into combat areas, swoop down and pick up the wounded, fly them back to the hospital, and then change her clothes quickly so that she could operate on them, because she was also a surgeon. ARE YOU KIDDING ME? The woman looks like she's fifteen in the picture. YOU CAN DO ANYTHING YOU WANT TO DO. What is it that you want to do? Almost invariably, whenever I ask that question of children who have gotten themselves into some kind of serious trouble, the answer is "I don't know." What they are really saying is "I don't have any idea whatsoever why some universal power has stuck me on this planet. It must be some kind of a cosmic joke. I am here by accident." No wonder you feel powerless. Find your purpose, find your power. I have a suggestion that might help. SMASH YOUR TV. SMASH YOUR GANGSTER CDs. Stop brainwashing yourself into being a violent, disrespectful idiot. Have faith in yourself that you can actually earn a good living and be helpful to others at the same time. YOU CAN DO IT.

I had a young man as a student who was the best welder we had seen come through the vocational school in a long time. He was on his way to making thirty-five dollars an hour, minimum. Young lady, what is eight times thirty? . . . . Remember that for me please. Young man, eight times five? . . . . And if I put those two together, what have I got? . . . . Two hundred and eighty dollars. That is per day, if the student had the ability to run his own business and weld for himself, and I believe he did. Anybody in here want to walk home with almost three hundred dollars? Every day? . . . . I thought so. One evening I got a phone call at my house from this young man, which I thought a little strange, since most students aren't so thrilled with school that they want to drag it out into the night. He apologized, but said that he was going to be absent for a while. I asked how long. When he responded three to five years, I realized that he was calling from the jail. He had shot into an occupied car when his midnight business transaction didn't go exactly as planned. What a waste. His life. My time. All because he didn't have any faith that game plan "A" was going to get him anywhere so he jumped to game plan "Z," what we refer to in the sports business as fumbling the football on the one yard line. Which leads to your other power source, that of character. Evidently intellect alone isn't going to cut it. Intellect without character will get you into trouble every time. Not only do you think you're smarter than anybody else, but actually SUPERIOR. You don't have to follow the same rules as everybody else. This is a seriously dangerous illusion, for both you and all the lesser human beings around you. Every single person in jail will tell you the same thing. I didn't think I'd get caught. The Enron boys sobbing how sorry they are? They didn't realize that others would take offense at them ruining the lives of hundreds of thousands of people? Oh, really?

Your character is your highest form of power. Intellect will get you a job. Character allows you to keep it. What is the first and foremost thing that a business person wants from you? It's not to do a good job. It's that you won't rob them blind when they are not paying attention. THEN, it's do a good job. The definition of character is what you do when nobody is looking. What, in fact, you really are at your core. Doing the right thing, all the time, to the best of your ability will get you places that strength and intellect can't even imagine. This idea is at the center of how the universe works.

I worked at a mental retardation center for a year and probably spent the first nine months wishing that they would call it something else. Anyway, I had a young man that we shall call John brought to me from somebody in the community. They wanted me to train him for a job that he was trying to get at a local fast food place. John was seriously challenged. He got "small" and "large" without too much of a struggle, but I thought that the concept of "medium" was going to kill us both. After snatching myself baldheaded, he was ready for work. The other thing about John is that he is, hands down, the nicest human being I have ever met. If a nuclear war had taken out the entire city, you would find John standing in the middle of the rubble with smoldering charcoal briquette hamburgers in each hand, a huge smile on his face, asking what he could do for you that day. He has kept that job for twenty years.

People can train skills, but it is infinitely harder to train character. That is going to have to come from you, and your view of yourself. Are you in this room because you are a bad person or are you here because you are a good person who is all too human and has down something bad? Is your condition permanent or temporary? That is the only question that really matters and the one that everybody in the human race needs to answer for themselves. What do YOU think of you?

Father Flanigan, who founded Boys Town, once said that there was no such thing as a bad child. I agree with him. That is not so important as whether or not YOU agree with him.

I am looking at a room of powerful people. What are you going to do with your new-found power? How are you going to deal with violence when it rears its ugly head? You need to come up with a PLAN. An anti-violence plan. If you don't have a plan, then you are going to fight. Guaranteed.

What did Ghandi and King do first? ORGANIZE. There is strength in numbers. Show some leadership. Combine intellect with character. If there is not a real, coherent plan in your school to deal with the specter of bullying and violence, demand one. Start one. Most schools have a violence plan, but it's not very good. It's called "Boy, that was horrifying and I hope it doesn't happen again." There is a concept called peer mediation, where students such as yourselves are trained to mediate conflicts BEFORE they turn ugly. There are teen courts. There are tangible reward systems for the use of nonviolence as a power tool. Start them. Use your student council as a real voice. VOTE. I am going to say that again, because it is the real power source that is available to everybody. VOTE. As a student. As an adult. There is a reason why untold thousands have been murdered globally in their quest for the right to vote. IT IS A REAL SOURCE OF POWER and don't let anyone tell you otherwise. They are not murdering and jailing people for the fun of it. The concept of one-person one-vote is a direct and dangerous challenge to the other concept of power, "Money talks and everybody else walks." Actually, it's "crawls," but that doesn't rhyme. There is one place and one place only where the rich and poor are equal and that is in the voting booth.

My suggestion is, if you don't exercise your right to vote, don't complain about NOTHING. If you are that lazy, then there is the reason why you've got a bunch of stuff to complain about. I learned several lessons while running for county commission, lesson one being whiners don't vote. They whine. At first I would listen to people's complaints for hours on end. "My road needs fixing. The taxes are too high. There are no jobs." Only afterwards would I find out that the last time they voted was for Dwight Eisenhower. Or better yet, they have never even bothered to register. If you guys want to brush up on your lame-o excuses for not doing your homework go out onto the campaign trail. There is a reason why some people live on lousy roads and are jobless. They even lack the creativity to come up with a lousy excuse.

If voting doesn't make you drunk with power then actually have the guts to turn off the TV and run for office. Don't look so shocked. Yes, YOU. Run for office at school, run as an adult. You want power, go for it. Not only is this not crazy, but it is actually doable.

I remember walking the streets with a young man, barely out of school, who had the insane notion of trying to become the first black Clerk of the Courts ever in my county. We would be walking door to door and I kept wondering what was that strange clacking sound I heard? I finally realized that it was his knees knocking. I recognized it because they made the same sound mine did when I went door to door during my quest for a county commission seat. He has been in office for years now with a wall full of plaques and accolades. I taught the sheriff in town when he was in the fourth grade. Even then he said that he wanted to be a police officer. He ran for office to become the first black sheriff in the history of the county. He's well on the way to being the best sheriff in the state.

If running for office isn't your cup of tea, have a dream and go for it. A friend of mine was the only female captain of a firefighting department in the state of Florida. If you dream it, and it is positive, and you are willing to work for it, it is do-able. You can make it real. Real power lies inside of each and every one of you. Have faith in yourself. Respect yourself. Don't be lazy. And don't fight. I mean, give me a break. Men, if you feel the need to prove your manhood, just take a quick look down your pants. It's there. You don't have to prove it. And fighting leads to undignified scenes. I saw a young man who was trying to fight while holding his pants up. There is a reason why professional boxers use both hands. Being knocked out with your pants around your ankles is not going to win points with your girlfriend, trust me on this one.

Leave the fighting to HBO. Go on and be a success in life so that you can afford to buy the over priced tickets. And go on home and hug your parents. They deserve one for what you've put them through. Enjoy the rest of your Saturday. At least the sun hasn't gone down yet. Class dismissed.

APPENDIX

Book reviews for "Bill Hoatson Presents "Professor Johnson's" Life Lessons."

"An Inspiring Journey Through Parenthood: A Review of "Bill Hoatson Presents 'Professor Johnson's' Life Lessons" by Bill Hoatson

Bill Hoatson's "Professor Johnson's Life Lessons" is a heartwarming and insightful exploration into the profound impact of parenting on child development. Drawing from his extensive experience, Hoatson delves into the crucial role parents play in shaping their children's lives, particularly during the formative years from birth to four.

Throughout the book, Hoatson shares invaluable wisdom gleaned from his observations and interactions with families over the decades. He eloquently illustrates how early childhood experiences lay the foundation for a child's future, emphasizing the significance of nurturing environments and supportive relationships in fostering healthy development.

One of the most compelling aspects of "Life Lessons" is Hoatson's compassionate approach to parenting. He acknowledges the challenges and complexities of raising children while offering practical advice and encouragement to parents navigating this rewarding yet demanding journey. His insights resonate deeply, reminding readers of the profound privilege and responsibility inherent in parenthood.

What sets "Professor Johnson's Life Lessons" apart is its blend of warmth, humor, and profound wisdom. Hoatson's storytelling captivates the reader, weaving together personal anecdotes, research findings, and timeless principles of child psychology. Whether you're a new parent seeking guidance or a seasoned caregiver looking for fresh perspectives, this book offers invaluable insights that inspire reflection and growth.

Moreover, Hoatson's emphasis on the long-term impact of early childhood experiences serves as a powerful reminder of the enduring influence parents have on their children's lives. By embracing his teachings, readers are empowered to create nurturing environments where children can thrive emotionally, intellectually, and socially.
In conclusion, "Bill Hoatson Presents 'Professor Johnson's' Life Lessons" is a compelling ode to the transformative power of parenthood. Through poignant storytelling and profound insights, Hoatson invites readers on a journey of self-discovery and enlightenment, reminding

us all of the extraordinary opportunity we have to shape the future through the love and guidance we provide to the next generation. This book is a must-read for anyone who believes in the limitless potential of children and the profound impact of positive parenting."

-REBECA HOLEMS-

"Bill Hoatson Presents 'Professor Johnson's' Life Lessons" by Bill Hoatson is a beacon of wisdom and compassion in the realm of parenting literature, and its availability in every bookstore and library is paramount. This book transcends mere instruction; it embodies a heartfelt invitation into the profound journey of parenthood.

Hoatson's rich narrative, infused with personal anecdotes and insightful reflections, offers a treasure trove of guidance for parents at every stage of the journey. His emphasis on the pivotal role of early childhood experiences in shaping a child's future underscores the book's relevance and urgency in today's world.

What makes this book a standout gem is its accessibility and applicability to diverse audiences. Whether you're a first-time parent grappling with the uncertainties of raising a child or a seasoned caregiver seeking fresh perspectives, Hoatson's gentle yet empowering voice resonates deeply.

Furthermore, "Life Lessons" doesn't merely dispense advice; it cultivates a sense of community and shared understanding among its readers. By advocating for the importance of nurturing environments and supportive relationships, Hoatson fosters a collective commitment to the well-being of future generations.

In an age where parenting can feel overwhelming amidst a sea of conflicting information, "Professor Johnson's Life Lessons" serves as a guiding light, illuminating the path with clarity and compassion. Its presence in every bookstore and library ensures that this invaluable resource is readily accessible to all who seek it.

In conclusion, "Bill Hoatson Presents 'Professor Johnson's' Life Lessons" is more than a book; it's a lifeline for parents navigating the complexities of raising children. By making this book available in every bookstore and library, we affirm our commitment to supporting families and nurturing the potential of every child. Its insights are timeless, its message timeless, and its impact immeasurable."

-MARY WEST-

"Bill Hoatson's writing skills in "Professor Johnson's Life Lessons" are nothing short of exceptional, deserving recognition in the literary world. His ability to craft a narrative that seamlessly blends personal anecdotes, profound insights, and practical advice is truly commendable.

Hoatson's writing style is both engaging and accessible, making complex topics such as parenting and child development easily understandable to a wide audience. He has a gift for storytelling, drawing readers in with vivid descriptions and relatable experiences that resonate deeply.

What sets Hoatson apart as a writer is his authenticity and sincerity. There is a genuine warmth and compassion in his words, reflecting his deep empathy for the struggles and triumphs of parenthood. He doesn't just dispense wisdom from an ivory tower; he walks alongside his readers, sharing in their joys and challenges with humility and grace.

Moreover, Hoatson's writing is rooted in a solid foundation of knowledge and experience. His insights are informed by years of working with families and children, giving his words a depth and credibility that is hard to ignore. He seamlessly integrates research findings and academic principles into his narrative, enriching the reader's understanding without ever overwhelming them with jargon or technical language.

In a literary landscape crowded with self-help books and parenting guides, Bill Hoatson's writing stands out as a beacon of authenticity and wisdom. His ability to connect with readers on a personal level, coupled with his expertise in the field of child development, makes him a valuable voice in the literary world.

In conclusion, Bill Hoatson's writing skills are exemplary, and he deserves recognition in the literary world for his contributions to the discourse on parenting and child development. His genuine voice, engaging storytelling, and wealth of knowledge make him a writer worth celebrating and a source of inspiration for readers everywhere."

-KATNISS MEAGAN-

"I believe that Bill Hoatson's book on successful parenting is valuable for everybody, but especially for teenagers and young adults. Many children come from homes that didn't function so well, which will give them problems in the future with knowing what to do when they themselves become parents. Mr. Hoatson has a parenting guide that will break the cycle of a dysfunctional home and empower any parent to raise a successful child. Not only it is informative, but it is fun to read. Mr. Hoatson has had forty years of experience teaching children at all grade levels in economically challenged areas of North Florida and Southern Georgia and his experience is needed by those aspiring to raise children.

The other lecture by "Professor Johnson" is on the power of non-violence to live a successful life and is the endcap to his parenting advice. It is something that every young person should hear.

I think that "Life Lessons" would be an asset to any school, re-entry center or prison as a roadmap on how to turn children into successful, productive citizens. For a small book it packs a very large amount of information and entertainment. It is highly recommended."

-ALONZO HARVIN-
Parenting Instructor
Re-entry Coordinator
Federal Prison System – 15 Years